MY MERCEDES IS ~~NOT~~ FOR SALE

MY MERCEDES IS ~~NOT~~ FOR SALE

From Amsterdam to Ouagadougou . . .
An Auto-Misadventure Across the Sahara

JEROEN VAN BERGEIJK

Translated into English by John Antonides

BROADWAY BOOKS • NEW YORK

Published in the United States by Broadway Books, an
imprint of The Doubleday Publishing Group, a division
of Random House, Inc., New York.
www.broadwaybooks.com

Originally published in the Netherlands as *Mijn Mercedes is
niet te koop* by Uitgeverij Augustus, Amsterdam, in 2006.
This edition published by arrangement with Uitgeverij
Augustus.

BROADWAY BOOKS and its logo, a letter B bisected on the
diagonal, are trademarks of Random House, Inc.

Book design by Barbara Balch

Library of Congress Cataloging-in-Publication Data
Bergeijk, Jeroen van, 1965–
    [Mijn mercedes is niet te koop. English]
My Mercedes is not for sale : from Amsterdam to Ouagadougou
: an auto-misadventure across the Sahara / Jeroen van Bergeijk ;
    [translator, John Antonides].—1st U.S. ed.
        p. cm.
    Includes bibliographical references.
    1. Africa, West—Description and travel. 2. Bergeijk,
Jeroen van, 1965—Travel—Africa, West. 3. Mercedes automobile—
    Anecdotes. I. Antonides, John. II. Title.
DT472.B4613 2008
916.604'33—dc22

                              2007044621

ISBN 978-0-7679-2869-4

PRINTED IN THE UNITED STATES OF AMERICA

10 9 8 7 6 5 4 3 2 1

First Edition in the United States of America

Publication of this book has been made possible with the
generous financial support of the Foundation for the
Production and Translation of Dutch Literature.

FOR MY PARENTS

CONTENTS

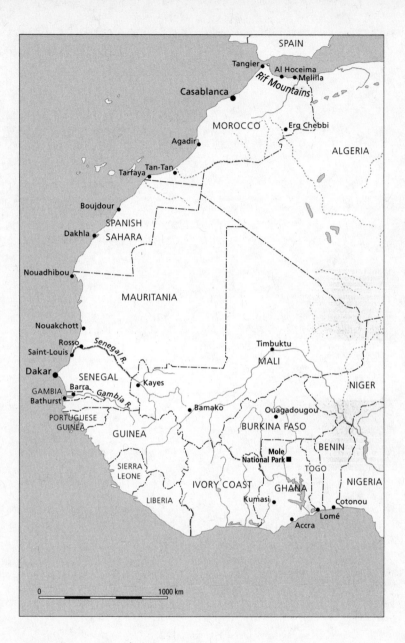

SPAIN

Tangier • Al Hoceima
• Melilla

Rif Mountains

Casablanca •

MOROCCO

Erg Chebbi

ALGERIA

Agadir •

Tan-Tan •
Tarfaya •

Boujdour •

SPANISH
SAHARA

Dakhla •

Nouadhibou •

MAURITANIA

Nouakchott •

Rosso •
Saint-Louis •

Senegal R.

Timbuktu •

MALI

Dakar •

SENEGAL

Kayes •

NIGER

GAMBIA   Barra •
Bathurst •

Gambia R.

Bamako •

Ouagadougou •

PORTUGUESE
GUINEA

GUINEA

BURKINA FASO

BENIN

SIERRA
LEONE

**Mole
National Park** ■

TOGO

NIGERIA

IVORY COAST

GHANA

Cotonou •

LIBERIA

Kumasi •

Lomé •

Accra •

0   1000 km

Oh Lord, won't you buy me a Mercedes-Benz?

—Janis Joplin

MY MERCEDES IS ~~NOT~~ FOR SALE

A MERCEDES IN OUAGADOUGOU

I don't think I ever would have thought of it myself. Visiting Ouagadougou, I mean. A good friend of mine, a fellow Dutchman, was getting married there, in the capital of the West African country Burkina Faso. To a *Burkinabé*. And I didn't want to miss that. The wedding lasted three days and three nights. The last night, exhausted, I hailed a cab. Now, Burkina Faso is one of the world's poorest countries, and I knew that most of the cars there are far from new. But this one had them all beat. The body was battered on every side, the headlights were missing, the tires, bald. Clouds of ink black smoke poured from the tailpipe. The interior wasn't much better: where once the odometer had been was now a gaping hole. Springs protruded through the seats. The upholstery on the doors had all but disappeared, leaving bare metal.

Stuck to the cracked dashboard was a decal of the Dutch soccer team PSV Eindhoven.

A PSV Eindhoven fan in Ouagadougou? I tapped on the team's red and white logo and asked the driver if he was an admirer of Dutch soccer.

He had no idea what I was talking about. He'd never heard of PSV, didn't give a damn about soccer. He didn't even know where the Netherlands was. And that decal had always been there. It looked it, too. Yellowed. Frayed at the edges—someone had tried in vain to pull it off. How had that decal wound up in an African taxi? Had the previous owner, perhaps, been a PSV fan? As fascinating as the thought was, a PSV fan in Burkina Faso seemed improbable. Wasn't it more likely that an even earlier owner had been a fan of the Dutch soccer team? That had to be it: that car came from the Netherlands. And sure enough, when I got out, my suspicions were confirmed. In Europe, every car has a white oval decal on the back with one or two black letters to indicate the car's country of origin: *F* for France, *S* for Sweden, *PL* for Poland, and so on. This one was no different: a white decal with the letters *NL* was stuck to the rear end.

It was a Mercedes 190 Diesel, that taxi in Ouagadougou.

THE PURCHASE

Year: 2004
Mileage: 136,400
Price: $1,200
Owner: Jeroen van Bergeijk

There are ads like this on the Dutch Internet auction site marktplaats.nl all the time:

> For sale: 1988 Mercedes 190 D
> Price: $1,400
> 136,400 miles. Alarm. Black 4-door.
> Excellent condition.
> Recent checkup, oil change,
> safety and emissions inspection.

This one gets my attention because everything about it seems right: the kind of Mercedes I'm looking for, a reasonable asking price, not too many miles, and a recent inspection. "My phone hasn't stopped ringing," the owner says when I call his cell phone number on a Saturday morning. "You can have a look, but the first good offer gets it." I drive immediately to one of the new suburbs just outside The Hague. The owner's name is Ronald. He works for the police. And so, the implication is, can be trusted. Ronald is a

3

well-built man with close-cropped hair, about what you'd expect for a police officer. Taciturn, a bit stern, but not unfriendly.

We stroll to his Mercedes, which seems rather out of place among the brand-new gleaming mid-class cars parked on Ronald's tidy little street. The finish is dull. There's a crack in the bumper. The sunroof doesn't open anymore. The driver's seat sags, and the doors don't lock.

I couldn't get that cab in Ouagadougou out of my mind. On the plane home to Amsterdam, I'd obsessed about how that car had wound up there. I imagined a Dutch aid worker who'd gotten the Mercedes from his uncle and imported it through the port in neighboring Benin. Maybe an African immigrant to the Netherlands had bought the car and sent it to his family in Burkina Faso. Or some adventurous Dutchman had driven that Mercedes 190 straight through the Sahara to Ouagadougou to sell it there to the highest bidder. But what really happened? How *did* a Dutch car end up in Africa?

Take Ronald's Mercedes. A seventeen-year-old car is, in fact, living on borrowed time: the average life expectancy of an automobile in Western Europe is only fifteen years. For a car like Ronald's there are really only two scenarios. Most likely it'll end up on the scrap heap. Not because a seventeen-year-old car is in such bad condition but because the cost of the repairs it will soon undoubtedly need will greatly exceed the car's value. In Western European countries like the Netherlands, Ronald's car has lost its usefulness. But in countries where the cost of repairs is much lower, the same car is still worth something. Hence the other scenario for Ronald's Mercedes: export. Of the more than seven million cars driving around on Dutch roads in 2005, more than a quarter million had been exported by the end of the year. All the wealthy Western European countries export their old automobiles, millions in total.

Nowadays most go to Eastern Europe, but a considerable minority, an estimated 500,000 per year, wind up in Africa. That Dutch Mercedes in Ouagadougou is not alone. The Opel Astra of a traveling salesman from Hamburg spends its days as a bush taxi in Ghana. The Toyota Corolla of a Parisian housewife is now the property of a camel trader in Mauritania.

Most of the old automobiles that leave Europe for Africa are shipped by boat, but a small number are driven there. In fact, since the 1970s, driving a used car to West Africa has become a popular pastime among French, Belgian, German, and Dutch adventurers. These people are like the godwits, terns, and swallows that summer in Europe. Every winter they flock to West Africa, selling their castoffs at a tidy profit in countries like Mauritania, Mali, Niger, and Burkina Faso. To get there, they have to bribe customs officials, befriend corrupt cops, and—above all—drive straight through the Sahara.

I go for a test drive in Ronald's Mercedes. It appears to have few mechanical problems: the engine runs well, the brakes are in order, and though the acceleration is a little sluggish, it shifts easily. It looks a bit shabby here in this brand-new suburb, but for a seventeen-year-old car it's in excellent shape. Ouagadougou's cabbies will envy me. I even get Ronald to knock two hundred dollars off the price, and a little later it's mine, that African-taxi-to-be.

"OKAY, THAT WON'T WORK"

At the motocross track down by Amsterdam's western docks, the whining of dirt bikes never stops. The sky is slate gray. It drizzles off and on. The track is half-covered with weeds and young willow trees. It's not the Sahara, but there is sand, and that's what counts. I'm here with Ruben and Raoul, who are going to teach me how to drive an ordinary automobile through loose sand. Ruben is a mechanical engineer, and he's already driven across the Sahara four or five times. He wears oversize glasses. He knows all there is to know about cars. Raoul is the owner of Off-Road Adventures, a company that rents Land Rovers and organizes "team-building events" in the Ardennes region of Belgium at which participants master some of the finer points of vehicle control. Raoul has a big mop of curly hair, wears a macho leather jacket, and is a huge fan of the Rolling Stones. His dream is to one day drive in the

7

Paris–Dakar desert rally. He's been preparing for it for years. The problem is it costs an enormous amount of money; professionals easily spend a few million on it. Even if you want to do it on the cheap, you still have to plunk down a couple hundred thousand, and Raoul doesn't have that kind of dough.

Raoul has brought along one of his Land Rovers today. To pull my Mercedes out of the sand if something goes wrong. Ruben and Raoul's teaching method is simple: practice makes perfect. I can figure it out myself. They set me behind the wheel, duck in the backseat, and have me drive onto the track. Very, very carefully, I drive through the sand. What happens next is something I've seen many times when my little boy plays in the sandbox with his toy cars: the wheels get stuck. The sand fills the space between the wheels and the body of the car. I don't go thirty feet before the engine conks out.

"Okay," Raoul says, "that won't work."

There are three things you should do when driving through sand. Downshift in time, maintain speed, and let air out of your tires. The last runs counter to intuition and to the advice drivers receive from their mechanic and their owner's manual: always keep your tires inflated to the prescribed pressure. But Raoul takes a dime, sticks it on the tire valve, and—hiss!—lets the air escape. Ruben makes a drawing in the sand with a stick. He sketches a tire deflated on the bottom. A tire flattened like that provides greater contact surface between tire and sand. The tire grips better and slips less. A fully inflated tire offers little contact surface. In loose sand, a full tire begins to slip, digs itself in, and—voilà—the car is stuck.

"It's a misunderstanding that you can only cross the desert in a four-wheel drive," says Ruben. "An ordinary car with soft tires does just fine." The great advantage of off-road vehicles is not that they're driven by four wheels instead of two—although that helps—but that they ride high on their wheels. There's considerable space between the ground and the chassis, the so-called ground clearance. If you leave the road in an ordinary car, which has little ground clearance, you're likely to damage something. For instance, a rock can tear a hole in the gas tank or the oil pan—the reservoir for the motor oil. On the street or highway, you experience few difficulties from little ground clearance. You actually only notice anything if you drive too fast over a speed bump. An off-roader laughs at speed bumps and other rough pavement. In a word, if you keep a sharp eye out for big rocks and don't do anything crazy (like driving through sand dunes), then, according to Ruben, a trip through the Sahara in an ordinary car shouldn't present too many problems.

When all the tires have been deflated, I try to drive on. In vain. "If we dig the sand away from around the tires, it should work," says Ruben. "And grab your sand ladders," he adds. Sand ladders are flat pieces of metal as wide as a tire and about five feet long. With plates like these under your wheels, you get extra grip. I bought two of these heavy, rusty pieces of iron at a Dutch army dump for less than fifteen bucks. I fetch them from the luggage rack and jam them under the rear wheels.

A little later Ruben slides behind the steering wheel and shows how it's done. He pulls the driver's seat all the way forward so that he's sitting practically with his nose against the windshield. He shifts quickly into second gear and gives it lots of gas. The engine screams, but Ruben doesn't touch the gearshift. He doesn't even slow down for the curves. The sand spatters high in the air. My palms sweat, my head hits the ceiling again and again, I have the feeling the whole time that we're about to turn over, that the engine's about to die. But we don't get stuck.

After a few more times around the track, I'm allowed to try it again. Then, slowly, I get the hang of it.

That evening at Raoul's place Ruben shows me photo albums of his Saharan trips. Lots of pictures of desert landscapes, his traveling companions, and, of course, cars. He points at a photo of a rusty Citroën 2CV, an odd-looking French model that became as popular in Europe after the war as the Volkswagen Beetle. The car's drivers stand beside it: two nonchalant, unshaven young guys in need of haircuts. "These guys had no idea what they were doing," Ruben says. "They were out of money. They had car trouble. Stood by the side of the road waiting for someone to come along who could help them."

I study the photo. Hip sunglasses and torn jeans. They're not my type, but I actually admire these guys. That they could take off just like that, without a care in the world. Without any preparation whatsoever. That they could just throw caution to the wind. That they could, in a word, surrender to fate. That's Africa, I muse: taking life as it comes, living for today, and not worrying about tomorrow.

As if reading my mind, Ruben blurts out, "With me, everything's got to be arranged. I don't wanna depend on anyone. You should always make sure that you can take care of yourself, that you can fix your own car." I hear pride in Ruben's voice. I appreciate his desire for autonomy. I understand his contempt for these irresponsible adventurers. But still, don't I also hear a bit of envy? Wouldn't he secretly, just like me, also like to be so easygoing, to let things happen—instead of preparing himself for every possible disaster? When I pose the question, Ruben stares at me with raised eyebrows, and to underscore that he finds the idea absurd, he grabs a piece of paper and a pen and begins methodically composing a list of things for the car that I should take along:

Red warning triangle
Five quarts of oil
Wire
Bar of soap
Towrope
Jumper cables
Tools
Jack and lug wrench
Set of filters (air, oil, fuel)
Electrical connectors
Duct tape
Zip ties
Flexible electric cord
Spare bulbs
Fuses
Panty hose
Hose clamps
Forty-six-ounce juice can
Three five-gallon jerricans for diesel
One five-gallon jerrican for water
Funnel
Two spare tires
Metal sand ladders
Shovel

A bar of soap? A pair of panty hose? A forty-six-ounce juice can? Ruben may not want to leave anything to chance, but he's not exactly rigid in his thinking. If you drive over a rock and get a crack in your gas tank, then you can fill the crack for the time being with an ordinary bar of soap. You tie a pair of nylon panty hose over the air intake to keep sand out of the engine. And should the exhaust system need fixing, you can do that fine with a juice can.

Patching up your car with soap, panty hose, or juice cans; the systematically compiled shopping list—Ruben's methods remind me at once of Robert M. Pirsig's classic, *Zen and the Art of Motorcycle Maintenance.*

The narrator and protagonist of that book is apparently a born technician. He writes computer manuals for a living. But he's not only a technician; he's also a philosopher—in fact, his book has little to do with motorcycle maintenance but is instead an attempt to synthesize the philosophical traditions of West and East. The book's leading thread is a motorcycle trip the protagonist makes from Minnesota to California with his son and two friends. Just like Ruben, the protagonist prefers not to depend on others. He maintains and repairs his bike himself. Not only that; he also takes pleasure in it. For him, a motorcycle is a machine first and only then a means of transportation. The romance of motorcycle riding—the Harley-Davidson feeling, say—seems to mean nothing to him. The protagonist enjoys understanding the logic of the bike's operation.

His traveling companions John and Sylvia, on the other hand, don't want anything to do with the motorcycle's technology. Worse, they hate technology. They're two classic hippies (the book originally appeared in 1974) who divide the world into "square" and "groovy." Square—that's the establishment, the middle class. Square is boring, respectable, rational. Groovy is the counterculture, the hippie. Groovy is exciting, wild, romantic. Motorcycles are groovy, but their maintenance is simply square. For John and Sylvia, the motorcycle is definitely a means of transportation, a thing to take them from point A to point B, to help them experience the world. They don't want to know how the thing works. Nonetheless, the protagonist does his level best to interest John in his motorcycle's maintenance. Time and again, he explains how important it is to understand something about your bike. John has every reason to do so: he's riding a BMW, and you won't find a mechanic who knows anything about German motorcycles any-where in the American Northwest. Should he need replacement parts or a repair, he'd be in a pickle. But John's solution consists in simply putting all thoughts of mechanical disaster out of his mind. Every time the protagonist brings up the art of motorcycle main-tenance or especially the need for it, John immediately tunes out. John's response is connected to his worldview, which is based on contempt for technology, for "The System." According to the nar-rator, he himself, the technician and philosopher, is interested in what things *mean*, and John and Sylvia are interested in what things *are*. They're Zen; the narrator, motorcycle maintenance. They, the Eastern philosophical tradition; the narrator, the West-ern. It's the antithesis between what Pirsig calls the *classical* man-ner of thinking, which is concerned with rationality, facts, and cause and effect, and the *romantic* manner of thinking, which is based on inspiration, imagination, creativity, and intuition.

The beautiful thing about *Zen and the Art of Motorcycle Main-tenance* is that Pirsig demonstrates that motorcycle maintenance is both the one and the other. It's rational but also creative. One day, the handlebars of John's BMW start slipping. Tightening a few nuts doesn't help. But the narrator has the solution: an empty beer can. You can cut a piece out of it and use it as a shim to help tighten the handlebars again. John, the pure romantic, is not only dissatisfied with that solution; he's offended as well. The idea that you could fix an expensive brand-new BMW with an old can is unbearable to him. The reason, the narrator explains, is that John has been seeing the shim in a different way: "I was going at it in terms of underlying form. He was going at it in terms of immedi-ate appearance. I was seeing what the shim meant. He was seeing what the shim was."

That's why I'm so impressed with that juice can of Ruben's. Because I recognize in him someone who sees the beauty of improvised, creative solutions. Someone who wants to understand what things *mean*. I'd like to write here "a kindred spirit." But do I really feel so connected to the approach of the narrator of *Zen and the Art of Motorcycle Maintenance*? Do I see my car in terms of its underlying form and not in terms of its immediate appearance?

Well, no.

Fix my Mercedes with a juice can? I think that's a wonderful idea. But that's all it is to me: an idea. I have to work awfully hard to immerse myself in this car's technology. I've bought a German repair-and-maintenance manual for the Mercedes 190 from the series *Jetzt helfe ich mir selbst* (Now I Help Myself) expressly for this trip. Ruben and the narrator of *Zen and the Art of Motorcycle Maintenance* may read such books for pleasure; every time I try it, I quickly nod off.

In fact, I'm just as interested in my Benz's immediate appearance as in its underlying form. Just as fascinated by what it is as by what it means. I could have bought a Toyota Corolla to drive to West Africa; that's just as popular there as a Mercedes. But a Toyota . . . that's hardly, well, groovy, is it?

Toyota's image is unequivocal: a boring but tough-as-nails automobile. Takes a pounding. That's why it's so popular in Africa. But Mercedes, that's a make that elicits conflicting feelings. Is a Mercedes a pimpmobile or the ultimate in refinement? Does the brand connote glitter and tastelessness or elegance and sophistication? Is the Benz neochic or genuine chic? For most of my friends, it's not too difficult: Mercedes clearly belongs to the former category. It's a parvenu brand that evokes irrevocable images of aggressive Amsterdam taxi drivers, a group, I believe, to which no sane person would want to belong. My friends are undoubtedly right. Why, then, do I want to drive a Mercedes so bad?

MY FATHER'S MERCEDES

The company car of Hooimeijer and Sons Ltd., manufacturers of baked goods and rusk, the peculiar toastlike bread that is a staple of the Dutch diet, was a Peugeot 404. A white one. Reliable, inconspicuous, cheap. The president of the company, my father, had no chauffeur. He drove himself. Actually, that Peugeot wasn't a company car at all, just our family car. But I do think the Hooimeijers considered it a proper choice. Joost Hooimeijer, the last owner-president from the Hooimeijer family, was an austere, religious man, a Calvinist in word and deed who at my father's appointment in the early 1970s gave him the Dutch equivalent of the King James Bible. "This compass was presented to G. P. van Bergeijk at the change of helm," he wrote in it. Ostentation was foreign to the Hooimeijers.

My father was perfectly happy with his plain Peugeot. He drove it for years with complete satisfaction.

But when a British multinational took over the company in 1973, it spelled the end of Dutch sobriety. An everyday French mid-class car like that didn't project the sort of image they had in mind in London. The simple Hooimeijer cookies-and-rusk company had to grow; other businesses were being taken over left and right. And according to London, the president of a modern company like that had to have a Big Car.

The choice fell on a Mercedes, an orange 240 Diesel.

My father hated that Mercedes with a passion. Not because he was ashamed to drive such a flashy car. In fact, my father had always wanted to drive a Benz. His uncle had become a millionaire in the grain business and would drive by my grandpa's bakery in the village of Hardinxveld now and then in a prewar Mercedes. What a fantastic car that was. What a battleship. One day I'll drive a car like that, too, my father, still a boy, secretly swore to himself. Now it had finally come true, and what happened? His Mercedes made a terrible racket and accelerated poorly to boot. "Sporty driving"—you could forget about it with this car. At a stoplight he'd always gnash his teeth as every other car beat him off the line. The thing just didn't have any pickup, and that tormented my father, a fidgety man.

My dad wasn't the only one dissatisfied with the Mercedes. My mother thought it stank of diesel. And of the sickly smell of vomit. I don't know what it was with that car, but my two brothers and I always got carsick when riding in it within half an hour. Only rarely did my father succeed in pulling the Mercedes over in time.

My one brother, the middle child, was ashamed of the Mercedes. Like most kids, he wanted nothing more than to be exactly the same as the rest of the neighborhood. We already lived in a big house; now we had a big car as well. "What am I supposed to tell my friends?" he asked my mother. That his father drove such an expensive car—he couldn't live that down.

My other brother, the oldest, was not only ashamed of our Mercedes; he was opposed to it as well. At the start of his senior year in high school, he refused to get in the car anymore. My brother, a hippie with long hair, a tattered jeans jacket, and a beard, saw in our Mercedes the symbol of a "corrupt capitalist society" and wouldn't be caught dead in it. From that moment on, outings with the whole family were no longer possible without a quarrel first. Only under the most vehement protest would my brother let himself be transported in that "pigmobile."

And me?

That Mercedes of my father's, the first Mercedes I ever rode in, had a sunroof. Sometimes, on a quiet road, I was allowed to stand between the front seats and stick my upper body through the open roof. When my father stepped on the gas, my back was pressed against the sharp edge of the roof. My eyes began to tear. My hair flapped in the wind. Those rides weren't long. A few hundred yards. But during that minute or two, elevated above my family, elevated above the world, I felt free. I wanted only one thing: to drive a Mercedes myself someday.

A year later, the diesel was traded in for a model that ran on gas. That was more like it. My father could accelerate, my mother could breathe, my one brother overcame his shame, and my other brother abandoned his opposition: he got a girlfriend in the big city, and then a driver's license and a father with a Mercedes came in handy.

A decade later—we had continued to drive Benzes all those years—I, too, was finally allowed to take driving lessons. Our entire village learned to drive at the same driving school, run by the De Jong family, which everyone called the Bontekoe family because the father and his two sons all had black bangs with a snow-white lock (*bontekoe* being Dutch for "spotted cow").

I had lessons on Friday afternoon; Bontekoe listened to gospel radio and sang along with the hymns at the top of his voice.

Besides hymn singing, he had two other great passions: eating her-ring and gambling. One week we'd stop for a herring—he knew the best herring carts in town—the next, for a cup of coffee in a snack bar. There, he'd easily gamble away twenty dollars in ten minutes. When I asked whether that wasn't against his religion, he shrugged. There's nothing in the Bible about that, he assured me.

Whether it was the distractions of the hymns, the herring, and the gambling or my own incompetence, the driving did not go smoothly. According to Bontekoe, I couldn't do anything right, was always dreaming, was too careless, failed to pay attention to what was going on around me. It was a year before I was permit-ted to take my road test. By that time, Bontekoe had long since given up hope of turning me into a decent driver. He had lost all interest in me, but my father's car—that was another matter alto-gether. He drove a boring Opel himself. Whenever the Mercedes was parked in our driveway, Bontekoe would pause to take a look at it and caress the roof, sighing. After a year and a half and three attempts, I finally got my driver's license. My father had sold his Mercedes only the month before.

"ONE HUNDRED PERCENT QUALITY GUARANTEE"

My girlfriend asks, "Now, how exactly do you think you're gonna manage there?"

My father shakes his head when I tell him what I have in mind.

The man at the garage lists all the things my Mercedes needs: new tires, new motor mounts, new brakes, new . . .

Kissing my girlfriend and our little boy good-bye, I leave on a cold, foggy December morning and immediately long for the sun, for the hot African interior. But the south will have to wait. First north, to Bremen, Germany, to the place where my Mercedes was made. The Mercedes-Benz factory in Bremen is huge, with its own exit on the Autobahn and nine different entrances. It churns out a thousand cars a day. My Mercedes rolled off the line here on April 26, 1988.

I'm curious about my car's birthplace, but I'm especially interested in how a Mercedes is put together, or, as Robert Pirsig would say, in its underlying form.

There's a line waiting at the entrance to the Mercedes-Benz Information Center, a big, gleaming colossus of glass and aluminum. The guy in front of me, about fifty, a little overweight, a look of anticipation in his eyes, has a German license plate tucked up under his arm. His hair is the same color as the car he's about to pick up: silver gray.

Mercedes offers its customers the option of picking their car up at the factory themselves. If you bring your own plates, you can drive the car right out on the road. Cars don't come any newer than that. *Werksfrisch*, Mercedes calls it—factory fresh. But before that, the owners-to-be get a tour of the plant. They hail from every corner of Germany, some even from England and Austria.

There are, of course, men with mustaches and gold watches, chain-smoking guys in their fifties with comb-overs, and older couples where the husband has a beer belly and the wife is dripping with gaudy jewels. But I also spot a couple of twentysomethings in fashionable suits, a kid with a red and white Mohawk, and a woman in cowboy boots. Here in Bremen it seems that Mercedes owners can't be so easily pigeonholed. Sure, everyone here is rich and white, but other than that there is little unambiguous to say about the new generation of Mercedes owners.

The auto plant in Bremen dates to 1938. It was built by Carl Borgward, a legendary carmaker, capitalist, and Nazi (who was locked up for three years after the war for employing POWs in his factory). Borgward's greatest claim to fame was the Isabella, named for his wife, which Germany's auto enthusiasts still consider one of the best postwar cars. But in the early 1960s, when he named a car after his daughter, things went wrong. The Arabella was a failure.

A little more than a decade later, in 1978, a competitor, Mercedes-Benz, took over the factory.

One of the first models Mercedes-Benz made in Bremen was the 190, the first "compact" Mercedes. After the oil crisis of the 1970s, Mercedes realized that it couldn't keep making only big, luxurious, gas-guzzling cars. On account of the high oil prices, the public wanted economical automobiles. The future belonged to the mid-class car. Mercedes spent nearly two billion dollars and ten years developing one, and all those years the press went wild with speculation. How would that "little" Mercedes look? The secrecy surrounding the new model, dubbed the "Volksmercedes" by a German auto magazine, piqued the public's curiosity. Fuzzy spy photos of the prototype 190 taken with a telephoto lens appeared in car journals all over Europe. Some magazines even ventured composite drawings, as if Mercedes-Benz had committed a crime and had to answer for it in court.

The Mercedes 190, also identified by its factory code, W201, in order to distinguish it from a model of the same name from the 1950s and 1960s, was introduced in 1984. The sales brochure exulted that the company had "succeeded for the first time, without compromises or concessions, in concentrating the famous Mercedes quality and efficiency in a compact automobile." The brochure touted the car's favorable "drag coefficients" and phenomenal "negative roll radius."

What it boiled down to was that the Mercedes 190 excelled at economy and maneuverability. Thanks to a new suspension system, the 190 held the road like a train. The Dutch magazine *Autovisie* grumbled that the acceleration was slow and the engine lacking in power but concluded nonetheless, "A nice car, the Mercedes 190 D. Doesn't immediately excel on the performance level, but quiet, economical, and with road-hugging qualities worth mentioning." If the Dutch were primarily impressed with the car's technology, the English-language press was full of praise for its design. The British *Road and Track* spoke of "an avant-garde design of pronounced forms and rugged lines." *Automobile Magazine* in the United States wrote, "The Mercedes 190 has flair while others have flash, style while others have fashion."

The 190 was a hit. By 1988 more than a million had been sold, many to people who had never owned a Mercedes before. In total, 1,879,629 Mercedes 190s would be made before production was stopped in 1993. At its introduction in 1984, the standard model cost twenty-three thousand dollars. *Autovisie* concluded accordingly that it was "reserved, unfortunately, for the wealthy of the earth." Twenty-five years makes a world of difference, for nowadays the 190 is the Third World car par excellence. Nowhere will you find more of them than in West Africa, one of the poorest regions on earth. An aid worker I would meet there later even thought the Mercedes 190 had become the perfect poverty indicator: the more 190s you see driving around, the poorer the country.

The tour is starting. The Mercedes owners are into it; they're as excited as a bunch of kids at a birthday party. We walk over a system of gangways high in the factory's rafters. Far below us, we see and hear the bustle of hundreds of clattering, crackling robots assembling Mercedes bodies. These robots are no chrome-plated monsters with blinking lights and high, thin, halting voices. Rather, they're big tentacles, supersized dentist's drills. One tentacle picks up pieces of steel, welds them together with an intense flash of light, and passes them on to another tentacle. I had imagined that the frame of an automobile consisted of only a few big parts: the chassis, a few side panels, a roof . . . and then you have a car. Something like that. But a budding Mercedes is a 3-D jigsaw puzzle: thousands of little pieces that have to be fitted together. The parts lie in enormous bins labeled with reassuring substantial-sounding German names like *vorbereitete Dachrahmen* and *Verstärkung Scharnier unter links*. The largest part is the size of a traffic sign; the smallest, no bigger than a credit card. You can't say that no human hands are involved in the manufacture of a Mercedes body—personnel shuffle here and there among the robots—but people here do primarily the dumb work. The robots put the bodies together; the people are only there to refill the parts bins.

"At Mercedes-Benz, we speak of a 'one hundred percent quality guarantee,'" says our guide, a waggish Irishman named Andrew Faust who has lived in Germany for years. It sounds like hype to me, so I ask him what he means. Everything is inspected, reinspected, and inspected once again during the entire production process, he says. The welds, the metal, the nuts and bolts—everything is checked by computers. Then daily a few bodies at random are pulled off the line and examined entirely by hand. The Mercedes-owners-to-be nod with satisfaction.

I've never in my life bought a new car. The pleasures of picking out a lease vehicle are foreign to me. Until I began this book, I'd never even been in an auto dealer's showroom. To tell the truth, I assumed that you bought a car the same way you purchased a washing machine. You walk in a store and say, "Gimme that one," and a week later it's delivered to your home. But that turns out to be the case only with the cars I can afford: used ones. With new cars, it works like this: you walk into a dealership, pick out a car, and then *it's made especially for you.* There isn't a single car made at the Mercedes factory in Bremen that hasn't already been sold. Every Mercedes embryo that glides by on the assembly line here already has an owner. But that doesn't alter the fact that you have to wait almost as long for a new Mercedes as you do for a donor organ. A Brit from Leeds says he's been waiting more than a year and a half for his new SLK Roadster.

Andrew rattles off trivia: the average Mercedes consists of some six thousand parts welded together at five thousand different points; more than eleven hundred pounds of steel go into it; and nearly seven gallons of paint are sprayed onto it. And so on and so forth: tens of thousands of people work here; per year thousands of tons of steel are handled by hundreds of robots. But none of it means much to me. I ask him how present production methods differ from those of the late 1980s, when my car rolled off the line. The difference is one of degree, Andrew says. Even then there were robots. Even then computers controlled the production process. Even then cars were made to measure. Only now there are more robots and more computers, and more cars are produced in less time.

Whereas more robots than people are involved in the manufacturing of a Mercedes body, it's just the opposite with the finishing of the car. In a factory hall farther on where the cars are completed, dozens of workers stand at the assembly line. The cars glide by continually. The dashboard is placed in the body by hand, as are the seats, the upholstery, and the windows.

Andrew isn't the only one partial to statistics: the company tries to inspire its personnel with all sorts of numbers. Enormous digital scoreboards along the line keep careful tabs on the employees' performance.

It's currently taking three minutes and twenty-two seconds to put an engine in a car.

The assembly line is running at a speed of an inch and a half a second.

Three hundred and twenty cars have already rolled off the line today (ten more than yesterday at this time), and another 277 are still to come.

The intent is clear: to give the factory workers as much information as possible about the progress of the production process in order to stimulate their enthusiasm for work. Their job satisfaction is, in fact, high. They even look contented. It could hardly be otherwise: a permanent job with Mercedes-Benz is still truly permanent (the typical Mercedes-Benz worker stays with the company twelve years) *and* well paid. And then, of course, there's that irresistible fringe benefit: the chance to buy a Mercedes at discount.

After four days and nearly fourteen miles on the assembly line, a Mercedes is ready. At the end of the line, next to the last factory hall, is a small racetrack. The turns are sharp and tilted at forty-five degrees. One in every ten new autos—from station wagons to speedy sports cars—is tested here. The test drivers tear over the winding course at speeds up to 120 miles an hour. Andrew speaks admiringly of the circuit. He calls it a "thrill ride." Once he accompanied a test driver. He got out after five minutes, sick as a dog. "The average Mercedes owner uses maybe 5 percent of his car's potential," he says. "You can do so much more with a Mercedes than just drive to work." It strikes me as a pompous remark, but I'll think back often on it later.

The tour is over. In the Information Center showroom, the new cars, all either black or silver, await their new owners. The owners are called one by one, and a salesman explains how each car works. With a simple C-Class he's done in five minutes, but for the SLK Roadster of the Englishman from Leeds he needs a full half hour. As the explanation progresses, the Englishman begins rubbing his face with his hands. His wife has spaced out already within five minutes. They jealously eye the German couples who, one after the other, have left with their Mercedes station wagons in no time.

It's time for me to leave as well. What, I wonder on my way out, is Mercedes-Benz's secret? Why is Mercedes-Benz "one of the world's best automobiles," as Andrew, with obvious pride, told me just now? Is it the high tech of the robots? Is it the low tech of the hands-on finishing of the car? Or precisely the combination of those two? Is it the factory's efficiency? The quality control? The attention to detail? The contented workforce? Or is it simply good marketing? I don't know. You could say it's all of this, but that, I think, is no answer at all. Surely Mercedes must have a defining characteristic. There must be something that makes Mercedes the car of choice among cabbies from Amsterdam to Ouagadougou.

Maybe I should consult Robert M. Pirsig again.

According to Pirsig's *Zen and the Art of Motorcycle Maintenance*, there are two ways of contemplating reality: the classical and the romantic. What I've seen here in Bremen is the classical manner of looking at a Mercedes: the screws, the engine, the technology. I've quite literally observed the Benz's underlying form. On the other hand, my youthful longing to drive a Mercedes represents the romantic manner of viewing the car. But those two approaches don't have to be diametrically opposed. There's a concept that rises above the contrast, Pirsig says, and that's "Quality." What exactly *that* is, Pirsig never really manages to explain, but frankly, as far as I'm concerned, he doesn't have to, either. I can get along just fine with this pronouncement: "To an experienced Zen Buddhist, asking if one believes in Zen or one believes in the Buddha, sounds a little ludicrous, like asking if one believes in air or water. Similarly, Quality is not something you believe in, Quality is something you experience." And that's exactly what I decide to go do: experience the Quality of my Mercedes.

TRICKSTER IN THE RIF

I take the Autobahn, the Route du Soleil, and the Autopista del Mediterráneo and drive without a break from Bremen to southern Spain. I'm not the only one fleeing the cold of northern Europe. In a restaurant parking lot not far from the Spanish resort town of Benidorm, I spot my first fellow desert travelers: Austrians on their way to Mauritania with a couple of gleaming SUVs. They're carrying sand ladders and jerricans on the roof. The drivers are bearded guys about forty years old dressed in cargo pants. Inside the restaurant, I tell them I'm planning on crossing the desert just like them.

"Look, there's my car," I say, pointing out the window at my Mercedes in the parking lot.

"Where?" one of them asks.

"There, that Mercedes," I say.

He looks at me, questioning. "You want to drive *that* through the Sahara?"

I shrug.

"Sure," I say. "That's a good car, you know."

The Austrian's face betrays a mixture of incredulity and indignation. They're two attitudes I've encountered before, though not with Andrew in Bremen, mind you. Andrew hadn't blinked twice when I told him of my plans. "Why not?" was all he said. Africa frightened him, but my Mercedes didn't worry him in the least. It would reach its destination, all right. I did find that mixture of incredulity and indignation in other travelers to Africa, however. In the months before I left, I'd spoken to dozens of people who'd traveled across Africa by car. Although some of these "overlanders" greeted my plan with enthusiasm, an equal number regarded me with thinly veiled contempt. The idea that I, in a seventeen-year-old jalopy, was going to undertake the same trip as they, in their SUVs plastered with decals for their Web sites and equipped with satellite phones, onboard navigation systems, four-wheel drive, and enough food for three months, rubbed them the wrong way. They considered me an irresponsible adventurer.

In Málaga, Spain, I board a ferry for Africa. Well, almost. Geographically, Melilla may be located on another continent, but officially it's still part of Europe. Melilla is a Spanish enclave in Morocco—just like the more westerly situated Ceuta. The crossing is really just a short trip within Spain; you don't even have to show your passport. You do feel like you've left Europe, however. The ship is packed; there's not a seat to be found. Moroccan children dance on the tables, tug at their mothers' skirts, and scream themselves hoarse. White tourists look up, annoyed; the Moroccan parents don't see anything wrong. We, the whites, want quiet and privacy; they, the Africans, bustle and conviviality.

Melilla has been in Spanish hands since 1497, and to Morocco's chagrin Spain still has no intention of giving it up. All sorts of things are smuggled in and out of Morocco here, especially drugs and people. Melilla is, together with Ceuta, the place where Europe borders directly on Africa, and it stands to reason that Africans try to get into Europe here. The ten-foot-high fence topped with razor wire is an insufficient deterrent. Africans seeking a better life in Europe storm the enclave on a regular basis.

The owner of Hotel Nacional is a Jew who, in addition to his hotel, runs an adjacent kosher restaurant. The man can't stand Moroccans. They're all *ladrones*—thieves—he confides. I'm inclined to agree. Early this morning, while I was sleeping, someone stole my car's side mirrors. That happens all the time here. At least that's what I gather from the fact that the mirrors of all the Benzes I see driving around are fastened to their frames with thick wire.

I spend the day wandering aimlessly, plucking up enough courage and enthusiasm to finally drive into Africa. A young man named Mustafa, who has downy hair on his upper lip and is wearing a polo shirt, khaki pants, and smooth light brown leather shoes, approaches me on the street. His eyes are bloodshot.

"*Woher kommst du?*" he asks in German—Where are you from?

"Amsterdam," I say, and he switches to broken Dutch.

I find that disarming. He has a brother in the Dutch city of Breda who owns a "coffee shop," one of Holland's famed hashish bars. Mustafa is in the car trade, and when I tell him I've arrived here with a Dutch Mercedes, he insists that we just *have* to have a drink together. I fall for it. I find his attention flattering. I haven't had a conversation in days that lasted more than a minute. We grab a table in Café Margello, his cousin's restaurant. Once we're seated, the first thing he says is that he hasn't worked a day in his life. Work is for suckers, for people who don't know how to make money an easier way. Mustafa has a sweet racket. He drives BMWs and Benzes to Melilla from the Netherlands and Germany. Here he sells the cars to Moroccans who transport them over the border illegally. Yesterday he sold a Mercedes 250 for seven thousand dollars.

Used cars are expensive in Morocco. The government sets sky-high import duties on automobiles—for my seventeen-year-old Mercedes, you'd have to pay about six thousand dollars. If you arrive in Morocco with a car, a note is made in your passport, and your license plate number is registered. If you leave the country without the car, you have to pay the import tax. Mustafa has found a way around this, but won't say what it is. He claims he can sell my Mercedes for three thousand dollars. All he wants in return is a modest commission.

It sounds tempting—a profit of 150 percent in little more than a week. Work is indeed for suckers. Mustafa orders mint tea and beer, talks a lot on his cell phone, and tries to pick up some Spanish girls in the meantime. I tell him I'd like to think his offer over. We arrange to meet that evening at eight o'clock.

At ten past eight, as I'm leaving my hotel, Mustafa comes walking up.

"Where have you been?" he wants to know.

He's been waiting for me at Café Margello with a friend, Dieter, a corpulent, pig-eyed German in his late twenties whose pink skin shows through his close-cropped hair. Dieter tells jokes like, "What do a taxicab and a queer have in common? You enter both in the rear." His eyes are just as bloodshot as Mustafa's. Dieter did a year and a half in prison in Tangiers—with twenty-six men to a cell—for smuggling hashish. His Moroccan business partners had ratted him out. There were two kilos of hash in the trunk of his Mercedes when the cops dragged him out of bed in his hotel. After telling his story, he asks me, "Wanna buy some stuff? Good shit, man. Top quality."

Although Dieter talks constantly, he doesn't look at me. He must have been a good-looking guy once; now his fat face spoils his appearance. I ask him what it was like in that Moroccan prison. He falls silent for a second. His face darkens, and he says, "Ah, *Scheisse*"—shit—only then to yell, "How do you get four queers on one barstool? Turn it over!"

Dieter has a Dutch mother who told him that Dutch is a coarse dialect of German. So naturally he doesn't speak a word of Dutch. But his best friend, Jantje, whom he met in the prison in Tangiers, does come from the Netherlands. Jantje, the owner of a pancake restaurant in the Dutch resort town of Zandvoort, did eight years for smuggling hash.

Dieter has been in Melilla a week. He was on his way to Morocco with a few friends for vacation but was turned away at the border by Moroccan customs. Morocco does not appreciate ex-cons. His friends went on; he stayed behind in Melilla. I don't really understand what he's doing here. Why take a vacation in a country that once threw you in a filthy prison?

"It's cheap here," he says.

We drink more beer. Mustafa wants to see the car and take it for a test drive. The three of us decide to go. They let me pay for the drinks. I've parked the car on the street. Mustafa thinks I really shouldn't do that. He wants to look for a parking garage. We drive around Melilla. Dieter lights up a joint.

"Hey, you know," says Mustafa, "it's no problem if you don't have any papers for the car."

We're lost. Mustafa says he has a house here, but he doesn't know the way. He does know how to get to the casino, though, and, what a coincidence, it's safe to park the car there. Mustafa and Dieter want to go in and gamble. Then it finally dawns on me that it's better to feign a headache and return to my hotel. Mustafa suddenly doesn't feel like gambling anymore and accompanies me there. As I shove the door of the hotel closed behind me, he sticks his foot in the door.

"Hey, man, can you loan me twenty bucks?"

Now I've had it with this trickster.

"*Ich zahle es dir morgen zurück*," he pleads in German—I'll pay you back tomorrow.

I feel like screaming, "Fuck off!" What a bullshit artist. This morning he had me believing he'd just sold his car for good money; now he wants twenty bucks from me.

"*Nein, nein,*" I mumble while trying to push the hotel door closed. "I really can't do that."

The Melilla border post is where Africa really begins. Thousands of people walk from Morocco to Melilla. Women lug baskets full of live chickens; men, heavy bags. Barefoot kids drive donkeys. A screaming man is walking in front of me. His only clothing is a torn pair of pants. No one pays him any attention, but everyone gives him a wide berth. Driving at a snail's pace, I try wriggling my car through the crowd. It looks scarier than it is. The Moroccan customs agents aren't very friendly, but they are efficient. I'm over the border in ten minutes.

The little town of Al-Hoceima lies at the eastern end of the Rif Mountains. At an outdoor café on Avenue Mohammed V— the Moroccan equivalent of Main Street (every hamlet has one)— a djellaba-clad young man with a long beard sits down next to me. I ask him the way to a hotel, and he replies, "You can speak Dutch here, you know." They speak Dutch in almost every restaurant and hotel. One in every ten cars has a Dutch license plate. It feels like the main Moroccan neighborhood in Amsterdam, or like Tilburg, another Dutch city where a lot of Moroccans have settled. A little later someone calls to me with a thick Tilburg accent, "You like Morocco?"

Outside Al-Hoceima, the Rif Mountains and the police checkpoints—a few barriers thrown across the road—begin. A policeman asks me if I'm here on "business." (Only later will I grasp the double meaning of that question.) No, for pleasure. He waves me on.

Moroccan drug dealers aren't stupid. You might think such gangsters would drive fast cars to outrun the cops: Ferrari, BMW, Porsche—brands like that. But drug dealers in Morocco have nothing to fear from the police: the authorities here have all been bribed. Cultivating hash may be a shaky business, but for transportation the dealers prefer genuine German reliability. All of them—really, all of them—drive Mercedes 190s.

Take the little village of Targuist, a few hours' drive east of Al Hoceima.

In 1957, in his essay "The Rif, to Music," the American writer Paul Bowles, who lived most of his life in Morocco, described the town as follows: "A monstrous excrescence with long dirty streets, the wind blowing along them, whipping clouds of dust and filth against the face, stinging the skin." Not much has changed in fifty years. The wind does indeed blow unusually hard—we're in the middle of the mountains here. Shish kebab is roasting over a wood fire by the side of the road. Pieces of lamb hang on big hooks. As I order a sandwich, a man named Ahmed comes up to me. He wears a cap and has a thick mustache.

"Holland people, good people," he opens the conversation. He's evidently seen my license plate.

I agree.

Ahmed is a cabdriver. He gazes admiringly at my Mercedes. He has a Mercedes himself. But it's out of commission, he says.

"You want business?" Ahmed asks.

"Business?" I ask. "What sort of business?" Would he perhaps like to buy my car? Ahmed explains what he means.

"*Travailler*. Business," he says. "You know." And he brings two outstretched fingers to his mouth and inhales quickly.

I shrug, and Ahmed starts to laugh. He can't accept that I don't smoke hash. That's impossible. Every Western tourist in the

Rif smokes and wants business. And that's good, because Ahmed is in the business. His father is in the business. Actually, his whole family is in the business. Ahmed wants to make my visit to the Rif a memorable one. He wants to organize a trip for me to a farm where cannabis is grown. I tell him I'm not interested and walk back to my car. Another 190 is parked next to my Mercedes. There are four unshaven men inside. They're acquaintances of Ahmed's. One of them rolls a window down. The man's appearance satisfies every cliché concerning unsavory criminals of North African origin. He has greasy hair, a three-day-old beard, a large scar on his cheek, and a filthy sweater. When he grins, he reveals large gaps in his teeth.

"Hello, my friend," he lisps. "You want business?"

I laugh, which the man takes as encouragement.

"Yes, business, my friend. Zero-zero. You want buy, yes?"

"Zero-zero?" I ask, but then I see what he means: the man displays a brick of hash the size of a thick paperback.

"Well, no, I don't need that kind of business," I say, then add with a smile, "but I have business for you. Wouldn't you like to buy my Mercedes?"

I regret that joke at once, because the four men jump out and swarm around me like bees around a hive.

"Yes, yes. Good car. Mercedes is the best," the driver exclaims enthusiastically.

He tries shoving the thick slab of hash in my hands, while the others attempt to get in the car.

I let the stuff fall to the ground—angry shouting ensues—and fight my way into my car.

With the doors still open, I tear off in the direction of Ketama.

Zero-zero, I later learn, is the best-quality Moroccan hashish. The champagne of cannabis, you might say. Actually, you could better compare it to extra-virgin olive oil. Zero-zero is made from the resin produced by the first processing of the cannabis plant. Ketama, on the other hand, is a popular, much lower quality, and therefore much cheaper Moroccan hash. What Thunderbird is to a wino, that's what Ketama is to the hard-core pothead. The *village* of Ketama is the legendary center of the cultivation of weed in Morocco. "A mecca for serious marijuana users," reports *High Times* magazine, the pothead's bible. Ketama is where the Moroccan trade in soft drugs began, and today it's a place where literally everyone is in the "business." Ketama is also a place many a curious hash tourist has considered himself lucky to leave without losing anything more than just his money and his luggage. *High Times* regularly publishes stories in which reporters barely manage to escape Ketama's drug gangs. Tourists dumb enough to buy hash here often end up in prison: the dealers maintain excellent contacts with the local authorities.

A few miles from Ketama, two Mercs, one dark red, the other black, stand at right angles to the road. As I pass, I see both cars pull onto the road in my rearview mirror, their wheels kicking up gravel. I'm being followed. There are goats and donkeys on the road, playing children, and women lugging bundles of branches. It's much too dangerous to drive fast, but I keep my foot anxiously on the gas. Yet it doesn't help: the dark red Mercedes pulls up alongside me. Four unshaven men again. They gesture for me to stop. I've got a good idea what they want and keep driving. Then the dark red car passes me while the black one comes right up behind me. The car in front stops, and I see in a flash in my rearview mirror that the black car wants to pull alongside. They're trying to box me in, I realize. I step on the gas and manage—for a moment—to escape.

This is no game. I'm beginning to get really scared. Not a minute later, I see the cars looming up again. They repeat the same maneuver. In the middle of Ketama, men in long robes with pointed hoods are crossing the street, as well as children trying to control a flock of goats. I have to swerve to avoid a stumbling donkey to which some sadist has tied dozens of jerricans. As soon as the passersby see my Dutch license plate, they begin shouting and gesturing. A boy pounds on my window. Someone tries to open a door. I'm driving too fast. Next thing you know, I'll kill man or beast. But what am I supposed to do? Let myself be robbed by a bunch of drug thugs? Shit, how long before I'm out of this lousy little town? Then, past the taxi stand and the mosque, the crowd of people thins out and I can accelerate again. Once more the cars try to overtake me, but then, suddenly, we drive into a patch of fog.

The dark red Mercedes gives up; a little later the black one does, too.

It's starting to drizzle.

"STRONG LIKE BULL"

Year: 2003
Mileage: 124,000
Price: $3,000
Owners: Ronald and Donna

I'd like to get to know my Mercedes the way you like to get to know new friends. You want to know who they are, what they've done in life. You want to know where they were born, with whom they've had a relationship, where they've lived, and what they've seen of the world. A friend—you can pour a couple of beers in him, and he'll start talking. But a car—you can only pour gasoline in that, and it still won't give anything up. How do I get to know my car's past? By speaking to its owners.

Ronald: "After you were here and said what you were planning to do—drive to Africa—I thought it over good again and came to the conclusion: Yeah, I think that car can handle it. The engine in that Mercedes was solid as a rock."

Donna: "You bet. That car was strong like bull."

Ronald: "I bought that baby in Priština, in

Kosovo, Yugoslavia. I worked for the UN there. I bought it from a local colleague, Anton, and he, in turn, had gotten it in Belgium. He told me a little old lady sold it to him. Yeah, sure, they always say that. There were more than 124,000 miles on the odometer. That wasn't altogether kosher, if you ask me. I suspect it was more like two and a half to three times that. I paid three thousand dollars for it, so, yeah, you could say I lost on the deal."

Donna: "We met in Kosovo. I was an interpreter-translator with the UN. People came to my mother and said, 'Oh, how terrible, what Donna's done, a relationship with an *international*.' They said, 'You can't get an Albanian, so you go with him.' "

Ronald: "We could never walk hand in hand when I was in uniform; we couldn't even touch each other. It's like the Turkish culture. You're supposed to reproduce within your own community. Maintain the 'race.' A rather primitive idea."

Donna: "I lived in Mitrovica during the war. The Serbians came and said we had to move out of our houses. We had to start walking to Albania. It was a five days' walk. There were thousands and thousands of people, in a long column. It rained. We had to sleep out in the open. We were beaten. They stole our money. I was together with my mother. My mother had made me very ugly. She had wrapped a big shawl around my head and said I should walk like an old woman. Women were dragged from the column again and again. Beautiful young girls. They were raped. But you could pay protection money. Five hundred deutsche marks, about $250. But even if you had paid, it began again a little later. When we reached the border, we couldn't go any farther. NATO had bombed the bridge to Albania at Djakovica. Then we had to walk back again five days."

Ronald: "Later her mother asked me, 'Would you drive us one more time over the route we walked then?' That's what we did. In the Mercedes. It was about fifty miles. I think it took us two hours."

Donna: "We couldn't return to Mitrovica anymore. Serbian people live in our house now."

Ronald: "It took us eight months to arrange a Dutch visa for Donna. We had made a couple trips with the Mercedes, to Macedonia and Greece. It held up well, and I thought: Let's take that car to Holland with us."

AN AUTHENTIC EXPERIENCE

I'm sitting atop an enormous sand dune in Erg Chebbi, a sea of sand in southern Morocco. This is exactly how I imagined the Sahara. A deep blue sky, a setting sun, golden yellow sand dunes as far as the eye can see. Here and there, gently swaying palm trees. It doesn't get any more exotic than this.

But . . . I'm not the only one enjoying the view.

I've been sitting here now for half an hour, and in that time four "caravans" of camels have trudged by. Loudmouthed French tourists in shorts sat astride the beasts. Later followed ten roaring motorcycles driven by tattooed men with flapping hair. A Swiss family arrived in a squeaky-clean Land Rover and settled on the dune opposite mine for a picnic. And just now two bright red motorized hang gliders flew over.

I console myself with the thought that the "real" desert is yet to come. Soon, in Western Sahara and Mauritania, I'll be rid of all these phony desert travelers.

But why, actually, do I think that? Why do I have to have the desert all to myself? Why is my experience spoiled by sharing it with others who are after precisely the same thing as me?

It all has to do, I think, with the objective every traveler pursues: an authentic experience. The traveler looking for an authentic experience is looking for places that have retained their "character." In practice, "authentic" often means untouched by modern life, by tourists and commerce. So it would be superauthentic to trek through the Sahara with a band of nomads and a camel caravan. There is a famous sign not far from here that appeals to that Western longing. It reads, "Timbuktu 52 Days." But modern nomads aren't stupid. They abandoned the nomadic existence long ago and now hire themselves out as guides and make good money putting tourists on camels. So that they can buy, say, a Mercedes and never have to ride a camel again themselves. Or, to put it another way, wherever you go in the world, sooner or later you run into other people, and then the party's over.

In his book *The Tourist Gaze*, John Urry argues that traveling is primarily a means of acquiring status. The longer and more exclusive the trip, the more status you acquire. The traveler is condemned to the desperate search for the last unspoiled place on earth, where the authentic experience—and the status—he so sorely craves repeatedly slip through his fingers. He journeys ever deeper into the world (West Africa) and goes to ever-greater extremes (driving an old car through the desert) to escape those annoying "others" and thus ensure his authentic experience. But what happens there on top of a sand dune in the Sahara, the most inaccessible, inhospitable, inhuman place in the world? The traveler fancies himself in Central Park on a Sunday afternoon. He sees his authentic experience—and his status—vanishing into thin air. That, then, is the real reason I'm sitting here fuming: my status has fallen.

Where did I go wrong? Where *should* I look for that authentic experience? Perched atop my sand dune, I page yet again through the *Lonely Planet*. The guidebook didn't warn me about this relentless desert commerce. Worse, it's mainly because of the *Lonely Planet* that I've come here. Wouldn't I have been better off leaving it home?

Well, no. Years ago—I was in my early twenties—I spent my summer vacations hitchhiking through Europe. Guidebooks were for tourists, I felt in those days. Books like that tell you where you should eat and sleep, what you should see, and then what you should think about it. But I wanted to figure that out for myself. No, I didn't need any guidebook. Consequently, I invariably wound up in either too-expensive mediocre hotels or cheap, horrible boardinghouses, ate bland meals, and visited the least-interesting museums. I squandered my time, and my quest for authentic experiences came to nothing.

Then I discovered the *Lonely Planet*.

If you wanted to have that authentic experience in three weeks, then you had to prepare yourself—that much had become clear to me. The *Lonely Planet* seemed made for people like me: young, individualistic adventurers on a tight budget. But above all for people who were wary of "tourism" and "really" wanted to experience a place. The name alone said it all. The lonely planet—that was exactly what I was longing for. But of course the *Lonely Planet* only exacerbated the problem it purported to solve: as soon as an exotic place, an affordable fine restaurant, or a cozy hotel was included in the guide, it was overrun by other *Lonely Planet* readers. *Lonely Planet travelers* could no longer be distinguished from *Lonely Planet tourists*. Good-bye, authentic experience—and, Urry would add, good-bye, status.

There seems to be no cure for this authenticity syndrome of the modern traveler. But there is. First of all, you can abandon the pursuit of authentic experiences. Stay home, in other words. Or, if that doesn't appeal to you, you can always become a tourist. But neither solution is very satisfying. And the urge to travel doesn't go away.

The best answer is to broaden the definition of what constitutes an authentic experience. Why should authenticity be equated with "untouched by modern life"? In *The Art of Travel*, a highly comforting book for any traveler, the author Alain de Botton looks for the exotic—which, I believe, is the same as the authentic—in the arrival hall of Amsterdam's Schiphol Airport. He describes enthusiastically how the sight of a sign there is enough to evoke a feeling of exoticism. Exoticism at Schiphol? The word "exoticism" sooner evokes associations with the things I see here in Morocco—palm trees, minarets, camels—than with a seemingly plain yellow Dutch sign. But exoticism is, in fact, nothing more than "different from home," and that sign at Schiphol was decidedly that for the Brit De Botton. The double *a* in *Aankomst* (Arrivals), the letters *u* and *i* next to each other in *Uitgang* (Exit), the use of English subtitles—all of which the Dutch themselves find so, well, prosaic—De Botton found it all exotic, or, if you will, authentic.

Authenticity isn't the same as "unspoiled by commerce and tourism." Exoticism isn't just veiled women and a camel caravan to Timbuktu. Authenticity is perhaps something more like Pirsig's Quality: you know it when you see it. It's not something you can believe in but something you experience. Authenticity has to do with the essence of a place or culture. The romantic in me says that the search for authenticity is not, as Urry would have us believe, a thirst for status but rather a longing to grasp the essence of a place. I know one thing: nomads on camels no longer belong to the essence of Erg Chebbi.

But then what does?

The *Lonely Planet* doesn't waste any ink on "Sahara Services." The tour guide Abdelkhalek—call him Abdul—thinks that's outrageous. Exulting, he shows me the latest edition of the *Rough Guide*—the Australian *Planet*'s British competitor—in which he *is* mentioned. However sparingly, his services are praised. It makes no difference to me. They're all annoying—the local tour operators who offer fully equipped desert camel excursions. Intrusive to the point of being aggressive, without exception. Abdul is a man with large brown stains on his teeth. He sits uncomfortably close. But he does speak decent English, and, more important, he knows what Western tourists want. I'm enticed by the tour he proposes: we'll drive a little ways into the desert in a Land Rover, travel farther by camel, and eventually spend the night in a nomad's tent.

That all sounds rather exotic.

Of course, the reality turns out to be a bit more prosaic. Our guide drops us off at a semipermanent tent camp. Diesel generators drone; a truck, SUVs, and a few tour buses are parked nearby. At nightfall, beneath that overwhelming starry Saharan sky, I see sparkling little lights on the horizon. Stars, I think for a second. But they're the campfires and electric lights of the dozens of other tourist groups that have settled here.

Abdul pokes at the campfire. Tea's on. Our hosts begin telling tales about their ancestors' legendary camel caravans. How the people trekked through the lonely desert for days on end and almost died of thirst.

Abdul launches into a soulful ballad.

But, hey, what's that? *Beep beep, beep beep*. Abdul's cell phone is ringing.

We're in the middle of the desert, but his cell phone is working as usual. It's a guy from his office, wanting to know when Abdul thinks he'll be back tomorrow morning. A new group of tourists is ready.

Has my authentic nomad experience vanished for good on account of that phone call? On the contrary. This *is* the authentic experience of Erg Chebbi. Abdul is the modern nomad from head to toe: he's out in the desert, under the starry sky, in touch with his roots . . . and with his office. I decide to throw some more frosting on the cake of this authentic experience. In the soft pinkish light of daybreak, I climb to the top of a dune, use my cell phone to take a picture, and then send it by phone to a few friends back home.

Of course, they *are* there, the minarets, the veiled women, the palm-covered oases, the bearded men in djellabas, the mysterious medinas, the boys on donkeys, the timeless souks, the wily rug merchants, and the pushy snake charmers. The old-fashioned, authentic Morocco—you need never look long for that. Nor for the modern Morocco, either, for that matter, although modernity still comes as a shock here—perhaps because the *Lonely Planet* and the *Rough Guide* don't write about it. Take Moroccan consumer society. Most of the visible economy is small-scale and informal, and brand names are still not common. You won't see a Wal-Mart, Sears, or Motel 6, and though every café serves the same espresso, no one yet seems to have a need for a Moroccan version of Starbucks. But there *are* exceptions. Gas stations and cell phones belong totally to the modern, Western world—you'll find a Shell gas pump or an outlet of the French cell phone company Méditel in even the smallest hamlet. And in downtown Casablanca, which looks like a drab 1950s public housing project in some Rust Belt city in America, I can't believe my eyes: there are roller skaters and bareheaded Moroccan women in tight jeans running around.

I'm in Casablanca to apply for a visa to Mauritania. The line at the embassy begins outside at the gate. I take my place at the end behind two Canadian girls, one with a pierced nose and upper lip, the other with bright red dyed hair. I also notice three light-hearted French fiftysomethings who plan on driving old Peugeots to Mali, a backpacker whose look betrays lots of Ketama, and a swearing, wildly gesticulating British tour guide who is getting herself extraordinarily worked up over the lack of efficiency among the Mauritanian diplomatic corps. Though the boorish Brit annoys me, I can't disagree with her. When my turn comes, after a two-hour wait, I learn that my black-and-white passport photos are no good. Photos have to be in color. Come back when you get them, I'm told. I'm still not used to it, the vaunted African rhythm, the patient waiting without knowing whether or when something is going to happen, the taking life as it comes without getting excited. I'm still too Western. It seems you can buy a visa at the border for fifty dollars. It's 1,240 miles from Casablanca to the Mauritanian border. I get in my Mercedes and start driving.

The plan is to follow the coast for 1,550 miles—through Western Sahara and Mauritania to Senegal—and then to travel overland into the West African interior. The Moroccan coast is green. Sloping fields, grazing sheep, orchards—it looks like Europe. Only after leaving the coastal town of Essaouira behind, do I notice the desert slowly approaching again. The brownish red soil is poor. Only the thorny argan trees thrive here. The trees are famous, and popular with tourists, because there are always a few goats in them. The goats climb to the top, eat the tree's fruit, and shit the indigestible argan nuts out again. The nuts are then made into a delicious oil that little boys sell by the side of the road everywhere here.

Just before the resort city of Agadir, in a bay surrounded by dark red rocks, dozens of surfers dash wildly to and fro, riding the breakers. It looks inviting, the tanned bodies gliding effortlessly over the tumbling waves. A tall young man with curly blond hair stands onshore taking a break. He wears knee-length pants and has a pair of fashionable sunglasses stuck loosely in his hair. His muscular upper body is bare. Peering out over the sea, he leans casually against his surfboard.

"You shoulda been here yesterday," he volunteers. "Much higher waves."

He's from Australia, and his name—I'm not making this up—is Bruce.

"Hey, Bruce," I say.

"Hey, dude," Bruce replies.

Within five minutes Bruce has told me his life story. "I live to surf," he says. He's been roaming the world for ten years, in search of that one "perfect wave." He gets a job now and then—he's just spent a few months as a bartender in London—but quits as soon as he's saved enough money to surf. "The English weather was driving me crazy," he says. "Someone told me they had good waves and warm weather here, and I left." He's staying here, near the little village of Taghazout, until his money is up. Another month and a half yet, he figures. And then? He'll see. Maybe South Africa. He explains patiently and at length how to surf, but when I ask why he surfs, he falls silent. "You know," he says after a while, "you'll have to grab a wave sometime yourself; then you'll have the answer to that question."

The waves are a few feet high today. Bruce, who is used to the waves in Australia, isn't particularly impressed. The village of Taghazout is a real surfers' colony. There are shops where they repair surfboards and sell surfer clothing—Billabong, O'Neill, Von Dutch. Jimi Hendrix echoes through the main street. Girls in bikinis sit in outdoor cafés. Bruce says hundreds of surfers live here. Like him, most stay a few months and then move on again. For the time being, Bruce, together with a couple of Germans, is renting a place hewn out of a cliff. Costs him a few dirhams. A villager provides dinner every evening. There's plenty of hash. There are waves. There's sun. What more do you want?

Indeed, what more *do* I want?

I'm jealous of Bruce.

"Relax, dude," he says. "Come along; I'll introduce you to my friends. You can see my cave. We'll smoke a joint . . ."

It sounds great. But I politely decline. My mission lies elsewhere. Not in this groovy Moroccan surfer life, but in the square, barren, lifeless desert.

And that's coming fast now. First, the grass disappears; after that, the trees; then, the bushes. Until only sand and rocks remain. Gone is the old-fashioned, authentic Morocco: the centuries-old casbahs have given way to gray concrete houses. Gone, too, are the symbols of the modern Morocco: the billboard cell phone ads adorned with seductive women have made way for giant portraits of King Mohammed VI.

Just past the little town of Tan Tan begins Western Sahara, the former Spanish colony occupied by Morocco since the 1970s. The United Nations thinks that the Sahrawis, the original inhabitants of Western Sahara, should decide for themselves if they want to be independent of Morocco, but it doesn't look like that's ever going to happen. The once so militant guerrilla movement Polisario, which is fighting for an independent Western Sahara, is hardly heard from anymore.

Morocco leaves no doubt at all as to who is in charge. At a distance of more than a mile, I count five enormous signs with royal portraits, including Mohammed VI as a soldier (in full-dress army uniform), Mohammed VI as a playboy (with cool hip-hop sunglasses and a big smile), and Mohammed VI as a serious statesman (looking dignified in suit and tie). From here on, Moroccan army checkpoints are as numerous as tollbooths on an American turnpike.

Two larger-than-life-size concrete camels on either side of the road into Tan Tan form an unofficial town gate. They seem to want to call to me: here is where it finally begins, that desert you've been looking for.

The two-lane highway turns off toward the Atlantic Ocean; the view now consists of endless arid plains to the left and endless sea to the right. The first sickle-shaped dunes appear on the distant horizon. So, too, the first free-running camels. Countless dead grasshoppers litter the shoulder. The penetrating stench of putre-faction makes me gag. Here, on the edge of the continent, the plague of locusts that has destroyed harvests in large parts of West Africa the past few months has come to an end. Wedged in here between water and sand, the insects couldn't go any farther and died en masse. There must have been millions of them.

Fine sand drifts over the asphalt in long strands. When I get out, it chafes my bare ankles. The visibility is getting worse and worse. It seems like fog. But it's extremely fine sand through which I can't even see thirty yards. It's the same brownish yellow powder I sometimes find on the roof of my car in the Netherlands—sucked up into the atmosphere by large storms in the Sahara, it falls to earth again only in northern Europe. I stop at a gas pump to pro-tect the Mercedes against the dust, tying an old pair of panty hose around the engine's air intake to keep the sand out. Another driver gives me a little grease to smear over my headlights. That helps pre-vent the sand from damaging the glass. Dust storms can sometimes be so violent that they scour your car's finish and glass totally bare.

No one describes the emotions that the barren, lifeless desert evokes more eloquently than the legendary French pilot and writer Antoine de Saint-Exupéry. I'm on my way to Tarfaya—or Cape Juby, as it was called in Saint-Exupéry's time—the place where he worked as the manager of an airfield in 1928. His stay there is re-flected in his most famous work, the novella *The Little Prince*, but also in the nonfiction book *Wind, Sand, and Stars*.

There was regular air service between Paris and Dakar as early as the 1920s—not for passengers, it's true, but for mail. Because airplanes had to be refueled often then, a lot of intermediate airfields were needed. Such as Cape Juby. Saint-Exupéry had a diffi-cult job here. He not only had to man Cape Juby's tiny airfield; he also had to remain on good terms with the Spaniards stationed nearby, who didn't take too kindly to the French, and was respon-sible for saving downed pilots as well. Although officially Spain ran the show, the native population took little notice. The Moors shot down many a plane, after which they tortured the pilot to death or, in the best case, released him for a huge ransom. It was up to Saint-Exupéry to see to it that the nomads didn't get their hands on the downed French airmen.

Saint-Exupéry complained about his lonely life in Cape Juby in letters home, telling how he only had someone to talk to twice a week, when a plane on its way to Dakar came by. "What a life," he wrote to his mother. "Like that of a monk, in the most remote place in Africa." He lived in a hut on the beach; his only compan-ion, the constant wind. A thin mattress, a washbasin with no wa-ter—those were, more or less, his possessions. The sand was everywhere: in his bed, in his food, in his clothes—that's why he always wore pajamas; all other clothing chafed his skin. Saint-Exupéry must have hated Cape Juby, but from his books you get the impression he'd found heaven on earth here.

Saint-Exupéry is a master at describing not so much the beauty of the desert as the state of mind evoked by its desolation. You feel connected to the earth in the Sahara. There are only three things here: wind, sand, and stars. And, oh, those nights. Saint-Exupéry's evocative descriptions leave you wanting but one thing before you die: to spend one night beneath the starry Saharan sky. "What is going on inside me, I cannot tell," he writes in a letter to his sister after a night in the desert. Saharan nights last forever, rekindling fond memories of youth. They have "a taste of Christ-mas" about them and engender a "light-hearted feeling." And that legendary love of Saint-Exupéry's for the desert, that passion for the ineffable beauty of emptiness—that began here, in Tarfaya.

I'd like to know more about that.

Tarfaya is an insignificant little town where the sand blows through unpaved streets. There is one restaurant and no hotel. Although Saint-Exupéry is by far the most famous resident the town has ever known, his name doesn't mean anything to anyone here. After asking around a lot, I finally find someone who once heard something about a French pilot who crashed here and never left. Yeah, that's right, he confirms, that Frenchman really liked it here in Tarfaya . . .

I'll just have to search on my own. The only tangible proof Saint-Exupéry ever lived here is a monument by the deserted beach, next to the former Spanish fort. It's a little green airplane that seems to have been made from some sort of giant Erector set and that stands on the spot where Saint-Exupéry once had his hut. The monument has no name; there's not even a plaque.

A mangy dog walks by.

Two boys in torn pants come begging a gift.

The sun's hot.

Black plastic bags blow across the beach.

I skip a few stones in the surf.

I lie down in the sand. I imagine how I'll fall asleep here tonight on the beach under the heavens and dream the stars from the sky.

Then a Moroccan soldier comes marching up to me. He's stationed in the half-ruined Spanish fort, now occupied by a Moroccan army unit. The soldier asks me what I'm doing here and wants to see my papers. Then he declares the area off-limits to foreigners, especially dreamy types.

Saint-Exupéry's work romanticizes not only nature but also people; he seems to have wholeheartedly endorsed the idea of the noble savage, man not yet corrupted by civilization. The Sahrawis are "fierce warriors" deserving of our respect. But did Saint-Exupéry really believe that? No. "They are thieves, liars, bandits; treacherous and cruel," he wrote his sister. "They kill a man as if he were a chicken." That was the case in 1928, and it was also true a century earlier.

In the forgotten classic *Sufferings in Africa*, Captain James Riley describes at length the atrocities to which the local population subjected him and his crew when they were shipwrecked off the coast of Cape Bojador, 125 miles south of Cape Juby, in 1815.

Cape Bojador, or Boujdour, as it's now known, was the end of the world in the Middle Ages. No ship dared sail past this "barrier of fear." The strong, cold southern branch of the Gulf Stream between the Canary Islands and the African coast inexorably ensured that every ship ran aground in Cape Bojador's shallow waters. It didn't become possible to navigate the rest of the West African coast until the Portuguese discovered a route around the Canary Islands in the fifteenth century. Nevertheless, in the centuries thereafter, countless ships continued to perish off the notorious Cape Bojador. Including the brig *Commerce* under Captain Riley's command.

After managing to reach shore in a lifeboat, Riley and his crew were immediately attacked by a group of Sahrawis. Leaving behind nearly all their provisions, they barely succeeded in escaping their attackers by again taking to sea, where they wandered about for a week. Within a few days, their water ran out and they began drinking their own urine—"a wretched and disgusting relief," according to Riley. There was only one thing to do: return to land. And as soon as they did, they were attacked again. This time they failed to escape and were taken captive as slaves. Riley and his crew were divided among several Sahrawi families and repeatedly resold—once for a blanket, another time for a water bag. They received scarcely anything to eat and survived mainly on goat intestines, camel urine, and now and then a little camel milk. Traveling through the desert naked and barefoot, they were horribly burned within days. Their skin hung from their bodies in folds. Their feet lay open to the bone. One evening Riley went looking for a big rock with which he hoped to beat his own brains in.

The desert around Boujdour has changed little since Riley's time. It still looks like a moonscape, a vast gray sand and gravel plain broken only by some pale rocks. A grounded ship, a recent victim of the still dangerous currents here, lies rusting in the Atlantic surf. There *is* a town now, with an Internet café where the proprietor is looking at a porn Web site when I walk in. But the people still live from camels; the animals are eaten here, and in the market you can even buy the slimy white fat from the hump by the kilo. Just outside of town I see a herd come jogging alongside the road at a trot. The camels are on their way to a well, where a few Sahrawis are watering the animals. The Sahrawis drop a big bucket in the well on a cable and hoist it up again with an old Land Rover. One of them tries to buy some diesel from me; another wants money for letting me watch him work. The wind is relentless. The Sahrawis have their faces wrapped up well in *cheches*, a sort of turban, but I feel the sand peeling the skin from my face. The sand gets in your eyes and hair—the latter feels like straw in half an hour. I don't yet feel like beating my brains in, but I am beginning to understand something of the despair of Riley and his men. I'm deliriously happy when I manage to retreat from the howl of the scouring wind to the comfort of my Mercedes.

Riley's lot only improved when he succeeded in winning the confidence of the passing merchant Sidi Hamet from Marrakech. Riley convinced him that he would fetch a lot of money in the more northerly situated port of Mogador, now Essaouira. In the eighteenth century, Mogador was the only town on the coast of what is now Morocco with extensive contacts with the West. Countries such as England, Denmark, France, and the Netherlands had consulates there. Hamet bought the captain and a few crew members from the cruel Moors, and together they made for Mogador.

Riley and four of his men were eventually ransomed by the English consul in Mogador. On arrival, Riley, who had once weighed more than 242 pounds, was only 88 pounds, while one of his companions weighed only half that. Two more crewmen arrived in Mogador a few months later; the rest of the crew were never heard from again.

Sufferings in Africa is much more than just an engrossing book that convinces by the perseverance of the characters and the harsh circumstances they manage to endure. It helped determine the course of American history. *Sufferings in Africa* was a best-seller in its time and made a big impression on the young Abraham Lincoln. It's said that in his youth the future president of the United States had just four books in his possession: *Aesop's Fables*; *The Pilgrim's Progress*; a biography of the first president, *Life of Washington*; and Riley's *Sufferings in Africa*. Some sources contend that it was this last book, together with a visit to a slave market in New Orleans at the age of nineteen, that formed Lincoln's ideas about slavery. It is, of course, ironic: a book in which whites are enslaved by Africans helped put an end to black slavery by whites.

THE GREAT VOID

The air over the asphalt shimmers. In the distance, the road disappears into the great void.

But the great void is a mirage. Because the asphalt actually disappears into the sand, into a sand dune to be precise. Okay, it's only three feet high, more a sand pile, but the three bulldozers trying to keep the road open are having a tough time with it just the same. This is the result of a weeklong sandstorm, one of the workers explains. He's been busy two days already cleaning up the mess. And when they're done bulldozing the road open here, they can begin again somewhere else. These bulldozers are like the pumps that drain Holland's polders, the dike-enclosed lowlands that the Dutch have reclaimed from the sea. They seldom stop; their battle against the elements knows no end. Come to think of it, it does seem a little like Holland here. Just as in the Dutch polders, tall power pylons are strung out along the horizon in one long line.

I keep thinking it can't get any more desolate than this; nature can't be any more brutal. But then I notice another crooked, nearly dead little acacia tree or a stubborn clump of grass. And that barren, deadly desert turns out to be anything but monotonous. Since Dakhla, the last town in Western Sahara, the white gray lunar landscape that began around Boujdour has changed into a sort of gigantic crème brûlée; the land bubbles and crackles as if on a grill.

It's not far to the border now. There, the blacktop ends and the sand driving begins. But first I need fuel. There's a little man by the only pump at the last gas station in Western Sahara. His eyes are hidden behind a pair of Ray-Ban sunglasses. He's wearing a bright blue robe and brand-new Nikes. He's missing a few teeth. His tanned face is deeply lined. I figure he's in his mid-fifties, but the I.D. he shows me says he's not yet forty. His name is Ismail, and he's a guide. He points proudly at the number in the upper-right-hand corner of the heavily handled scrap of paper: 1. He's Mauritania's first and oldest guide. This station is his base camp. He travels here every week to pick up tourists looking to drive across Mauritania. That's what I'd like to do, but not with Ismail. I think I'll make it without Ismail. I try to make that clear to him while filling my Benz's tank.

"Non, merci," I say a few times.

It makes no impression whatsoever.

"Are you aware there are mines near the border? The road's not blacktopped there," Ismail says.

Yeah, whatever, I think, exhausted.

With a copy of *Sahara Overland*, the Sahara traveler's bible, under my arm, I march across the lot to the station's diner, acting much more purposeful than I feel. I eat a plate of soggy fries and a piece of stringy chicken. Ismail never leaves my side. I show him the fist-thick *Sahara Overland*.

"I've got everything I need to know right here," I snap at him. "Really, thanks, but I don't need you."

Ismail looks at me and shakes his head.

I see him thinking: Book knowledge. Do you really think you can fathom the desert's mystery with a book? Do you really think you can cross the most inhospitable terrain in the world with that?

My destination is Nouadhibou, the second town in Mauritania, about thirty miles from here. The route to follow is described mile for mile in *Sahara Overland*. If I follow the directions exactly, I ought to arrive in Nouadhibou this very day.

Twenty minutes later I reach the Moroccan-controlled border post. A frayed rope hangs across the road. A customs agent sits sprawled in an easy chair. The agent, unshaven, cap on the back of his head, scrambles to his feet and saunters over. He walks around the car, and then says, "Haven't you got a beer for me?"

I laugh. "But that's forbidden, isn't it?" I say. "There," and I gesture toward the rope.

"Uh-huh," he mumbles in agreement. "If they catch you with alcohol there . . ." He doesn't finish the threat, and he doesn't have to, either. I know enough. Alcohol has been officially forbidden in the Islamic Republic of Mauritania since 1968. Under Islamic law, or sharia, the punishment for violating that prohibition is forty publicly administered lashes (diplomats and civil servants, by the way, are exempt from this compulsory abstinence; they can drink with impunity). Not that Sahara tourists are frightened by the law. Almost everyone has a supply of booze in the trunk. Me, too.

"No, sir, no alcohol," I say, lying.

If he opens my trunk, he'll find my stash of wine in a couple of minutes. To my amazement, he drops the subject. But I still can't drive on. First I receive another sermon about land mines, about the lack of asphalt, about the need to hire a guide who can lead the way. I listen with only half an ear, still glad the subject of alcohol is closed.

They told me at the gas station that the border in Mauritania shuts down at five, and it's a quarter after four now. If I don't reach the border, I'll have to spend the night in the no-man's-land between the two border posts—not a pleasant prospect.

"Can I go now?" I ask impatiently when the customs agent falls silent for a second.

He shrugs and drops the rope.

The blacktop ends after fifty yards. Before me lies a forsaken rocky plain. Rocky outcroppings stick up here and there like enormous pimples. The wind blows. Sand and dust obscure the view. Where I'd expected a clear path are only tracks fanning out in all directions. *Sahara Overland* is no help at all. Wherever I look, no matter how hard I peer, I can't spot the landmarks the guidebook describes. And worse: there's not another driver in sight. I'm rereading the chapter about the border area between Western Sahara and Mauritania when my eye falls on a note that says that tourists who have wandered from the route have perished in a minefield. Wandered from the route? What route? I can't think of anything better than simply driving straight on. The car immediately scrapes on a rock. Or is it a land mine?

Then the sand begins. I let up a little on the gas. It feels like I'm driving into soft butter. I hear the engine grumbling, downshift, and . . . the engine conks out. I start it again, try to drive on, but nothing happens. When I get out, I see that the wheels are sunk in the sand up to the axles. I've done everything wrong. My first stretch of sand in the Sahara and I'm stuck, can't go forward or back.

And there I stand, in the middle of a minefield. The border closes in half an hour. I have no idea where I am or what to do next.

It's hot. It's so hot you can feel the heat of the sand through the soles of your shoes. Then, seemingly out of nowhere, some men come trudging up. They look seedy, in faded jeans and torn shirts. What do they want with me?

"We'll help you," says one.

"We'll push," says another.

But that's not what I want. Stay calm. Approach the problem logically. Like a technician. What did Ruben say again? First, let air out of the tires. And so I begin with that.

"Now what are you doing?!" one of the men shouts.

"That makes no sense at all," says another.

I feel like crying. I feel like screaming that they should all just fuck off, but I hold my tongue. The wheels are already too deep in the sand. This no longer makes sense, yet I stubbornly persist. When I start the engine, I only make matters worse. The car sinks even deeper. Okay, then I just have to dig. I haul sand away from around the wheels, but whatever I do, I can't make a dent. Every time I toss a shovelful of sand aside, new sand slides back in.

"That's not gonna work," one of the men says.

Determined, I follow Ruben and Raoul's scenario: deflate tires, dig out wheels, then lay sand ladders under the wheels.

"Now you can push!" I yell at the men.

When I start the car and give it some gas, it shoots forward a little. Then it jolts again, and the wheels begin to spin, but I keep my foot firmly on the gas. Fine sand sprays in all directions. Suddenly I'm gaining speed. I'm free! When I'm back on solid ground, some twenty yards farther, and get out to retrieve the sand ladders, the men are shuffling away again.

But what now?

I need those guys. How else will I get out of this minefield alive? I whistle with my fingers. I blow the car's horn. Agonizingly slowly, one of them trudges back. He wants fifty bucks to take me to the Mauritanian border post.

I think: That's a lot. Really, under the circumstances, I hesitate. But I don't have much choice; I take out my wallet, and the man gets in the back. He lives amid the land mines, in the no-man's-land between Western Sahara and Mauritania. We drive past his home, a rubbish heap of engine blocks, overturned wrecks, and flapping tents. He lives off people like me, tourists who get lost in this no-man's-land or, better yet, have car trouble. Then he buys the stranded vehicles for a song, patches them up, and sells them in Mauritania for a sizable profit. We're at the border in five minutes.

"Look, there it is, behind that hill," he points. "I'd rather they didn't see me here." He opens the door and disappears.

I don't have to worry: no one's showing any signs of closing the border yet. The border post is a wooden shed. Inside are three rickety beds. A blanket with a floral motif lies on one. In a vain attempt to keep the sand out, someone has nailed plastic sheeting to the bare boards of the unfinished walls. A customs agent, a black man with a scarf tied round his head like some sort of improvised turban, sits drawing lines in a big book with a pencil and ruler.

"Just imagine," he says. "No, seriously. This evening. *This* evening. You could be standing at the airport in Nouakchott with fifteen hundred dollars in your pocket. Whatta you think of that? Back home again tomorrow. Not bad, eh?"

No, not bad at all.

I'd expected a lot at the Mauritanian border. Corruption, extortion, men with whips. But an expert used-car salesman?

"Eighteen hundred dollars. Nice price, eh? Come on now, two thousand."

The customs agent, dressed in army green, ignores my passport. He doesn't care that I don't have a visa. The car's papers don't interest him at all. What he wants is my Mercedes. And at any price, it seems. There's no objection he can't answer.

"But if I sell you my car, how do I get out of here?" I ask him.

"I'll take you to Nouakchott."

"But I want to travel farther, to Senegal and Mali," I counter.

"Then take the bus."

He won't quit. He flatters, he threatens, he offers cash on the barrelhead. And that last almost does it. He pulls a big wad of bills out of his pocket. "Look, that's for you."

Out of this dusty hell, out of this scorching heat, with two thousand bucks in my wallet.

Not bad at all.

When I go outside again, three Spaniards with a gleaming new SUV are standing there, along with a Dutch couple trying to get back to Morocco in an antique Land Rover. The Spaniards, bearded men in their forties with wraparound sunglasses and baggy pants, have been shaken down. They had to pay the man a hundred dollars. One of them had to surrender his cell phone. They're stunned. And how about you? they ask as I walk out sweating and sighing.

"Fifty bucks," I mutter, trying not to boast.

The deal-happy customs agent had given up after fifteen minutes. I didn't give in. Of course not. I've only just begun. Even if he'd offered me ten thousand dollars, I still wouldn't have sold. I've not even seen the real Sahara yet. After I slipped him that fifty bucks, he let me go.

The Spaniards consider whether they should ask for their cell phone back.

"It's probably because we're rich and you're not," one of them says.

The Dutch couple, Mariska and Hans, have stood by shaking their heads.

"You still don't give them any money," says Hans.

"Never in a million years," says Mariska.

Mariska and Hans have sunburned faces streaked with dirt. They've been traveling around West Africa half a year now. "Pay at the border? You don't do that."

Then a tall man on a bicycle comes riding up over the hot, sandy road. It's Anton, also from the Netherlands. He's six feet six with a flaxen beard. Sweat pours from his thin, muscular body. Anton is an unemployed farmhand. Nine months ago, he thought: I can do one of two things. Sit at home moping till a job comes along again, or go biking. A choice between stagnation and movement. He chose movement. The advantage of biking, he says, is that you don't spend anything. Sure, on food, but you have to eat anyway. He sleeps in a tent he pitches wherever he pleases. He's biked to Belgium, to France, to Spain, always farther south. Often 125 miles a day. Sometimes he called home to see if there was work. There wasn't, so he kept going. He caught the ferry to Morocco in the Spanish port of Algeciras and, just like me, sailed down the coast. But now, in Mauritania, something has changed. He doesn't think much of it here. You can't get a beer anywhere, and though he doesn't ask for much, a cold beer now and then would be nice. He doesn't like the people, and you can actually hardly bike in this country with all these bad roads. He's done nothing else for months but put distance between himself and the Netherlands, but yesterday, on the spur of the moment, he decided to return. He's headed home, closing the gap.

Anton has worked out the perfect strategy for passing borders. He feigns ignorance. *"No Français,"* he replies with a thick Dutch accent to the customs agent's every question—I don't speak French. The official leafs through Anton's passport. He eyes the Dutchman, amused. He wants twenty-five dollars from Anton, but the latter stubbornly persists, *"No Français."*

Pfff, the agent finally says, waving him away with a languid flick of his hand. Mariska and Hans, the three Spaniards, and I gaze at him admiringly. Didn't pay a cent. He sure handled that well, didn't he? I still have a million questions, but Anton has already mounted his bike again. I watch him as he slowly dissolves in the hot, shimmering air.

TUPAC IN THE DESERT

The streets of Nouadhibou are sandy; the houses, concrete. Emaciated goats eat plastic bags. Little grows here. No plants, no bushes, only here and there a pathetic, half-withered little tree. Rusty shipwrecks litter the beach.

I have a hard drive ahead of me, for all I know the hardest of the entire trip. I have to get from Nouad-hibou to Nouakchott, the capital of Mauritania. Three hundred and ten miles straight through the naked desert. *Sahara Overland* describes a rough trip consisting of sand roads, treacherous dunes, and a long stretch along the Atlantic beach where you have to look out for fast-rising tides. As I lie in bed at night, I have visions of having to dig the Mercedes out time and again, of the transmission falling out, and of waves devouring my car. But there are also reports about a new highway between Nouadhibou and Nouakchott. They've been working on this so-called

Trans-Sahara Highway for years, but now it seems to be finally nearing completion.

How should I continue? Not alone, that much at least is clear after those anxious moments in that minefield in Western Sahara. Back in Holland, experienced Sahara travelers had assured me that I'd have little trouble finding other people who, just like me, wanted to cross the desert in an old car. It's best to drive together with at least one other vehicle to Nouakchott. That's not only safer—if your car breaks down, you can always continue in another—but also more efficient: you can help push each other out of the sand. Traveling together was born of the desert code of conduct. Every Sahara guidebook mentions that you can never refuse help to a driver in need. If someone with car trouble is standing by the side of the road, then you stop and help him as best you can.

That's all very well and good, but in the meantime I've not yet succeeded in finding even so much as one traveling companion. I already tried once, in Western Sahara, at a campground in Dakhla. There was a Frenchman in his mid-thirties camping there who drives to Nouakchott four or five times a year to sell a car. He wasn't getting rich off it, he said, but he was managing to make ends meet. His breath stank of cheap wine, and the Peugeot 505 he was driving backfired like mad whenever he started it. I asked him what was so great about desert driving. He stretched his arms, acted as if he were steering a car, and began jerking the invisible steering wheel like an idiot. I met four German seniors at the same campground. They wanted to attempt the crossing in a motor home—a motor home!— equipped with satellite dish, chemical toilet, and refrigerator.

I was sure I'd find better company later.

A group of exuberant Frenchmen is sitting in Nouadhibou's Chez Momo inn. They arrived this afternoon with car trouble—a hole in the gas tank and a clutch that's acting up—but they don't seem worried about it. I find them congenial. I wouldn't say we hit it off, but we get along; they're okay. I hope to be able to join them, so I do my best to be likable. Thomas is a young version of the French movie star Gérard Depardieu: a huge body; greasy, long blond hair. Large gestures; loves rugby. His friend Maurice is a male nurse in a hospital south of Nice. Their African adventure has them both fired up. They pass around joints. Maurice has never been abroad before.

"So why all the way to Africa the first time, then?" I ask him. I like his answer. Rather than start in about adventure or "primitive cultures," he talks about improvisation.

"Nothing is what it seems in Africa," he says. "Nothing works like it ought to work, like it would work at home. We're gonna have problems on this trip. Hey, you know what? We've already had problems, with the car. What I wanna know is how I'll react when something really goes wrong."

Maurice reminds me of those two nonchalant young guys in their clunker Citroën 2CV in Ruben's photo albums. Intentionally maneuver yourself into an impossible situation and then just see. Maurice and Thomas are groovy, I decide. I think it might be fun to tag along with them for a while. They think so, too. They just have to put it to the rest of the group first.

In the meantime, I go looking for a garage that can mount a protective plate under the oil pan. The oil pan, the engine's oil reservoir, is the most vulnerable part of the car when driving in the desert. One big rock, and you've got a hole. All the oil runs out of the engine, and you can't drive any farther. Ruben had told me that, just as with a crack in your gas tank, you could repair a hole in the oil pan with a bar of soap, but I'd feel a little more at ease with a somewhat more substantial solution: a metal plate on the bottom of the car.

Momo knows a guy. Momo is Senegalese and proud of it. He has an extensive collection of Senegalese music cassettes. Baaba Maal, Ismaël Lô, and, of course, Youssou N'Dour. A framed poster of the Senegalese national soccer team, quarterfinalists in the 2002

World Cup, hangs above his bed. "*Notre succès et aussi le vôtre,*" the poster reads—Our success and yours, too. That's probably why the patriot Momo takes me to a countryman.

Momo's mechanic is named Amadou. I can't believe his workplace. There are mountains of junk—tires, cardboard boxes, rusty parts—and half-dismantled wrecks everywhere. Amadou has no office, no lift to put cars on. He doesn't even have any tools—he has to borrow them from colleagues across the street. He works in the sand, which is gray with oil. But mounting a plate under a Mercedes—that's child's play to him. He saws a square plate out of an old metal door, drills a few holes in it, and half an hour later my Mercedes is desert-proof.

The next morning Maurice and Thomas, looking glum, are forced to admit that their *chef d'équipe,* their team leader, doesn't agree to our traveling together. I ask this guy—a fool who's tied a blue *cheche* around his head, as if he could be overtaken by a sandstorm any second here in Chez Momo—what the problem is. He drove through the desert once, five years ago, and he thinks that makes him an authority.

"I do not wish to bear any responsibility for you," he says.

"An ideal expedition consists of three automobiles," he says.

"We would have a problem communicating," he says.

And then the real reason comes out. He doesn't trust my Mercedes. The Frenchman has no confidence in a German car. I can't believe my ears.

I've had it. I want to leave, so I ask Momo to arrange a guide. Within half an hour he's drummed up a young Moor named Sidi Ali. His I.D. says he's twenty-five; in reality, I think, he's just turned twenty-one. He wears a baseball cap and speaks a few words of French. I tell Sidi Ali what I'd like to do. I'd like to fol-

low the Trans-Sahara Highway under construction, sleep one
night in some idyllic little spot in the desert, and take my time.

"Pas de problème," says Sidi Ali.

I have my doubts. But what else can I do? It's either stay in
Nouadhibou even longer or leave with this kid now. It's stagnation
or movement. It doesn't take long to decide.

Within fifteen minutes, it's obvious I've made a mistake. Sidi
Ali is an annoying adolescent. He acts like he owns the world. He
blabs endlessly on his cell phone and only stops when his phone is
out of range. Without asking, he begins monkeying with my CD
player.

"Don'tcha have any 50 Cent?" he whines.

No. But to his immense delight, I do have Tupac. He tries
singing along phonetically.

"I am a nigger," the Moor jabbers proudly.

And that while he's just ordered me to stop the car so he can
throw a few stones at some impudent black kids. Sidi Ali smokes
like a chimney and refuses to open a window. Then the dust will
come in. When we stop to get something to drink, he quickly
grabs the keys out of the ignition and won't give them back.

"I'm the *patron*"—the boss—"now," he says. "Ask nice."

I'd like to slap him.

Sidi Ali knows no doubts. The world makes perfect sense.
Since he's such a fan of rap music, I ask him if he'd like to visit
America someday. No, he wouldn't. Mauritania is the best country
in the world, and he hasn't the slightest desire to go anywhere else.
My questions annoy him. When I ask about the things around
us—What sort of plant is that? How often does it rain here?—he
shrugs and looks at me as if to say, "What sort of stupid question
is that?" I ask him if he's afraid of the future. The Trans-Sahara
Highway is finally almost finished, and that'll just about elimi-
nate the need for guides. According to Sidi, that's not true. But he

knows just as well as I do how things stand. He doesn't want to admit that his living is threatened.

"Business is good," he says, and to underscore his point, he whips out the fifty-euro bill I gave him as an advance.

What really bugs me is that he doesn't make the slightest effort to please me. His only aim is to get me to Nouakchott as quickly as possible: he doesn't give a damn about the desires I expressed earlier. Sidi doesn't consult; he commands. Left here, drive on, step on it, now stop. And if my life depended on his judgment, I wouldn't object. But of the nine hours the journey ultimately takes, we drive eight on asphalt.

Really gorgeous asphalt, by the way, gleaming black with spotless white stripes. The Trans-Sahara Highway is indeed almost finished—the camel-crossing signs are already in place. Perhaps a little while longer and the only remaining obstacle will be the border area between Western Sahara and Mauritania. Should a solution for that be found as well, you'll be able to drive from Amsterdam to Dakar without ever having to leave the pavement. So there is every reason to believe that with this highway there will finally be a permanent, modern connecting road between Africa north of the Sahara and Africa south of the Sahara.

The desire for such a connection has existed since the end of the nineteenth century. In 1879, inspired by the construction of the Transcontinental Railroad in the United States, France conceived a plan to build a Trans-Sahara Railroad. The railway was supposed to connect Algiers, in the north of Algeria, with the French Sudan, an area roughly equivalent to present-day Mali and Niger. Whatever those Americans are capable of, they probably thought in Paris, mighty France can certainly do, too. Besides, France needed a prestige project to polish its tarnished image in the world. The France of Louis XIV and Napoleon was history; worse, France was still suffering the humiliation of its defeat in the Franco-Prussian War of 1870–71.

The Trans-Sahara Railroad was the brainchild of the engineer Adolphe Duponchel, a man who specialized in grandiose plans. He'd once proposed a pipeline between the Languedoc and Paris as an efficient means of supplying the capital with red wine! This dealer in harebrained schemes also wanted to use high-pressure water cannons to artificially erode the Pyrenees so that fertile soil would cover the Camargue wetlands in southern France. It's hardly surprising the French public never warmed to these ideas, despite their originality. Yet strangely enough, the proposal for a Trans-Sahara Railroad met another fate.

In 1879, in his book *Le chemin de fer trans-saharien* (The Trans-Sahara Railroad), Duponchel explained why such a desert railway was necessary and how it ought to look. Railroads, he argued, were forerunners of civilization. Lay down an "iron road" somewhere, and development would follow of its own accord. Thanks to the railroad, towns and cities would arise, communication would improve, and barbaric peoples would be exposed to the culture of the Western world—which, of course, could only do them good. That had all happened in America, and now it was Africa's turn. France would enlighten the Dark Continent. Imagine, Duponchel wrote: Paris to the tropics in only six days. Moreover, a railroad would give France access to the "riches of the Sudan" (what exactly those were, the author didn't say) while expanding the market for French products (as if the inhabitants of the Sahara were in need of perfume and Bordeaux, the two most important French exports at the time). So there were in fact no economic reasons; the Trans-Sahara Railroad was exclusively a prestige project meant to disseminate French culture.

Building the railroad would be a big job, but then again, Duponchel insisted, the difficulties needn't be exaggerated. The biggest problem was the lack of water—a steam train requires considerable quantities. Though years go by in the heart of the Sahara without a drop of rain, that could be solved by digging wells and installing pumps and pipelines. The problem of the constant sand-storms and "wandering" dunes that bury everything in their path would be tackled by cultivating plants.

Nor, according to Duponchel, was there much to fear from the native population. The Tuareg, who occupied the southern part of present-day Algeria, weren't nearly as bold as the Apache, and they, after all, had been nicely brought to heel in America. And besides, once the Tuareg saw what blessings the railroad would bring, they'd quickly abandon any resistance.

The author thought he'd find cheap labor, which had made the American Transcontinental Railroad possible, among France's work-shy youth. In one fell swoop, then, the country could also rid itself of all its undesirable elements. Paris thought it an excellent plan and made money available for research. Debate over the desir-ability of the scheme, let alone the feasibility, did not take place. All that remained was to send somebody out to chart the railroad's fu-ture course.

That task fell to Lieutenant Colonel Paul Flatters, a corpulent man with a neatly trimmed mustache who looked more like a banker than the Africa hand he was. Flatters had been stationed with the French army in Algeria more than twenty years. He spoke fluent Arabic and had published various historical and an-thropological studies of North Africa. Made for the job, you might say.

Unlike the politicians in Paris, who had let themselves be hoodwinked by Duponchel, Flatters knew all too well what great dangers his mission entailed. France controlled only Algeria's north; the south was unknown terrain where the mysterious Tuareg, relatives of the Berbers, held sway. For centuries, the Tuareg had lived off the murder, plunder, and extortion of caravans and solitary travelers. Few Westerners had ventured among them and lived to tell about it. One who had tried was the Dutchwoman Alexandrine Tinne. In 1869, after years of wandering around Europe and Africa, this stalwart society lady paid with her life for her attempt to become the first Western woman to cross the Sahara. She was robbed and murdered by her Tuareg guide. And Tinne was far from the Tuareg's only victim. The list of adventurers killed by the Tuareg in the decade preceding Flatters's expedition was considerable: all told, dozens of Catholic missionaries, French journalists, and German explorers. In a report written just a few years earlier, Flatters himself had concluded that the French could seize control of the Sahara only with an enormous display of force.

Nonetheless, he set out in January 1880 with just fifteen French soldiers and some seventy Bedouin of the Chaamba tribe. The expedition was plagued with problems from the get-go. An expedition like this needed a strong leader; what it got in Flatters was a man who always looked to compromise, an officer who tried to be pals with everyone. From the start, discipline in the ranks was practically nonexistent. Stealing and brawling were the order of the day. Flatters tried to keep peace by distributing gifts, but that only made matters worse. Shrewd traders in Ouargla, the expedition's starting point, had stuck the lieutenant colonel with all their sick and scrawny camels. One after the other bit the dust. The Tuareg got wind that Flatters was vulnerable. They dogged the expedition for days, pinched its supplies, and finally flatly refused it passage. Flatters ducked the fight and retreated—all the way to Paris. There he had to admit that the expedition, for all its expense, had produced nothing.

That should have been the end of the story, of course. But Flatters managed to convince the politicians in Paris that France's honor and reputation were at stake. A year later, a second expedition was mounted.

That expedition, too, consisted of fewer than a hundred men, although this time they were better armed. Once again, Flatters's lack of drive immediately manifested itself. He became paranoid, trusted no one, and fell prey to depression and violent bouts of temper. Moreover, he suffered from a severe form of sciatica: he could walk no more than thirty minutes at a time and only obtained relief from the pain by lying down. Incapable of making any decision, he withdrew more and more to his tent. Meanwhile, his guides worried about the camel tracks they were seeing. It looked as if groups of Tuareg were gathering and riding on ahead of the expedition. But on January 25, 1881, the tide seemed to turn. A Tuareg leader let it be known that the expedition was welcome and promised free passage. Two guides would accompany the group to the French Sudan. Flatters set out in good spirits. The guides led the expedition deeper and deeper into the desert. It got ever hotter and drier. Water became more and more scarce. Camels dropped dead; the men collapsed from exhaustion. Now and then, a few Tuareg would arrive in camp loudly demanding gifts, and if they didn't receive them, they'd help themselves. On the morning of February 16, 1881, the two Tuareg guides announced they were lost. Somehow or other, they'd walked past the well they'd been searching for for days. Flatters exploded in a rage. It was decided to pitch camp for the day and send a small group to continue the search for the well.

It turned out to be a trap.

The two guides led Flatters, a few officers, and almost all the camels to a canyon where a group of two hundred Tuareg with spears and scimitars stood waiting. There was no possibility of escape. Flatters and his men were massacred.

But the drama was still far from complete. Those who had stayed behind in the base camp, fifty-nine well-armed men, had survived. Instead of launching a counterattack in an attempt to get their camels back, they decided to retreat at once. The group began the return trip to Ouargla on foot, 930 miles, or seventy-five days' journey, to the north. Without camels . . . and without any provisions to speak of; in their haste, they'd had to leave those behind.

Some men deserted, others committed suicide, still others collapsed and were left to their fate. Slowly, systematically, inexorably, what was left of the expedition was further decimated by the Tuareg. One day the Tuareg gave the members of the expedition, emaciated and half-mad with hunger, a bag of dates—they turned out to be poisoned, and three men died. Another day they sold the group a portion of their own abandoned provisions—the men who came to the Tuareg camp to pick the stuff up had their throats cut.

Ultimately, the remaining members of the Flatters expedition degenerated to cannibalism. On March 22, three Chaamba Bedouin murdered one of their tribesmen and presented his bloody carcass to the rest of the group as that of a wild animal. No one was fooled, but they eagerly consumed the human flesh just the same. And with that the last shred of civilization had disappeared: in the days that followed, one half of the group slaughtered the other, and they ate one another raw. The Tuareg looked on, amused. Finally, on March 28, 1881, eleven half-dead Chaamba and one Algerian soldier stumbled into Ouargla. None of the French had survived. Nothing more has been heard of plans for a Trans-Sahara Railroad since.

But now there's the Trans-Sahara Highway. In fact, there are even two Trans-Sahara highways. This one here along the coast of the Atlantic Ocean and one that follows, more or less, the route Flatters had in mind: via Ouargla, In Salah, and Tamanrasset in Algeria to Arlit and Agadez in Niger. They've been working on that one for decades with no end in sight. But here in Mauritania it looks as if they're finally going to succeed.

Although . . . while the work is still going on, in some places the road surface is already crumbling away. Nets have been stretched along both sides of the roadway to hold back the blowing sand. But many of those nets have been torn by sandstorms. There are portions of the road where the new blacktop has already half-vanished under the first advancing dunes.

The problem, of course, is maintenance—like everywhere in Africa.

Things in Africa come in two forms: broken or almost broken. Whether it's the power plant or the water supply, the Internet café's computers or the city buses, the sewage system or the airport runway—seldom does anything in Africa work like it's supposed to work. The art of motorcycle maintenance? The art of any maintenance whatsoever is a completely unknown concept here. It's not that all Africans are groovy, that they're romantic thinkers, that they've not read Pirsig. No, the philosophy here is of a whole other order; the general attitude toward life is that of *inshallah*—God willing. If it's Allah's will that my cab fall apart, then that'll happen whether I maintain it well or not. So why should I care whether my brakes are in order and whether the tires still have sufficient tread if it's ultimately Allah who runs the show? But I don't really believe that religion is the true cause. I think you have to look for the explanation in the fact that in Africa the future does not exist. Each new day is a struggle for life—even apart from wars and famines. A great many Africans don't know in the morning if they'll be able to eat come evening, so why would they think of tomorrow? Why would they look any further than next week if they don't even know if they'll still be alive tomorrow?

One might object that poor maintenance in Africa is a consequence not of religion or a lack of a concept of the future but simply of too little money. Maintenance would come of its own accord if we, the wealthy Western nations, would just make sufficient funds available. Of course, the problem is, in part, a matter of money. If you have to choose whether to spend the few miserable cents you've earned today on food or on an oil change for your cab, the choice isn't hard. You choose for your growling stomach. You choose for now and not for later. But is it really that simple?

Take Amadou, the mechanic in Nouadhibou. When he mounted the protective plate under the oil pan of my car, I was struck by how dangerously he went to work. He placed my car on a jack that was hardly meant for the weight. The thing sagged and had obviously seen better days. It creeped me out, so I got the brand-new garage jack that I'd picked up just before I left out of my trunk. The thing can lift two tons. Amadou thought it was great. So I made him an offer he couldn't refuse. Or so I thought. In exchange for putting the plate under my car, I'd give him the jack.

No deal. Amadou preferred money. It wasn't that he had no need for the jack—he did, he said. Nor was it that he thought his work was worth more than the jack—he didn't try to negotiate the price. No, he needed money to pay his bills. Here he had the chance to invest: a new jack would guarantee the continuity of his business and at the same time be good for his safety. That old jack was the only tool he had. Without it, he'd be in trouble. And one thing was certain: that jack of his clearly belonged to the category almost broken. But Amadou didn't want my jack. He got his money and spent it.

Now, that was one thing. I could follow his reasoning. But then he asked: Can't you give me that jack? Here was someone who could take care of himself, who had mastered a trade, had his own business, and who shamelessly asked: Won't you give it to me? Like a little kid.

I think that Amadou's private problems aren't so very different from the collective problems of African governments. Just like Amadou, the average African state is weighed down by debts. Just like Amadou, the African state must choose between food for its citizens and investment in the future. And just like Amadou, the African state expects free help from the wealthy West (more than a third of the budget of a country like Burkina Faso consists of foreign aid). But would Amadou change if I gave him that jack? Will the African governments change now that their debts have recently been partially forgiven? Maybe. Or maybe they'll continue along the same lines in the expectation that they'll be bailed out again the next time, too.

In any case, I let my emotions govern my decision: it annoyed me that he began to beg, and I put my jack back in my trunk. That protective plate was first-rate, by the way.

"I WANT NOTHING BUT MERCEDES FROM NOW ON"

Year: 1999
Mileage: 93,000
Price: $2,750
Owner: Anton Cena

"I drove eighteen hours straight from Priština to Antwerp yesterday," says Anton Cena, the man who sold my Mercedes 190 to Ronald in February 2003. "Stopped for twenty minutes in Austria to get something to eat. I'm in shape. I'm an athlete."

Anton worked at the same police academy in Kosovo as Ronald. They even look a little alike. Anton, too, is short and stocky, with a muscular build and close-cropped hair. But while Ronald weighs his words, Anton wears his heart on his sleeve. "Did Ronald really sell you that car for twelve hundred dollars?" he exclaims incredulously. "No offense, but I'd sooner torch it than sell it for that. Really. That car was worth twice that. I drove that car close to seventy-five thousand miles. It was indestructible."

I meet Anton in an Antwerp neighborhood known as Borgerhout, where he lived for eight years and still owns a house. Anton is a native of Kosovo, but he speaks a hodgepodge of Flemish and English. He returns to Belgium once a year to attend to things and visit family.

Anton has good memories of my Mercedes, a car his brother picked up for him. "I once had an accident with that Mercedes of yours. You didn't know that? Well, okay, so I had a collision with a Volkswagen Jetta. I had a little damage: broken headlight, bumper fell off. But that Jetta! It looked like an accordion. My wife was trembling. I said to her: 'Mercedes is Mercedes. I want nothing but Mercedes from now on.' And just last week. There's a UN checkpoint near my home in Kosovo. They have those big bags piled there, filled with stone. They duck behind them when there's shooting. It was night. I heard a tremendous bang. Went to see what was happening. I thought someone had thrown a hand grenade. A kid in a Mercedes 190 had crashed into those bags. The car was totaled. But that kid didn't have a scratch. You know, those Germans are a little stupid. The cars they make are much too good."

I ask Anton how he wound up in Belgium.

"I was a major with the police in Kosovo. In 1990, all the officers had to sign a document, an oath of allegiance to Serbia. I didn't want to. So they kicked me out of the police. A few weeks later they began arresting all the officers of the police and army. I went to Croatia the very same day. I stayed there a year and a half. Then war broke out there, too. I was drafted. War is ridiculous. I don't wanna die for nothing. You go and fight, and then you die, and no one will remember you. Your wife and children are left behind without any money. No, that wasn't for me. I fled to Belgium."

In Antwerp, Anton started over for the third time. He earned a living as a dishwasher and a cook in an Italian restaurant on the Keyserlei, the main Antwerp shopping street. He bought his house in Borgerhout, his children were born here, he even became a Belgian citizen, but he never really felt at home. "I had it good here, but then again, I didn't. You know, the people here don't like foreigners. I'm a foreigner, too, but I agree with them. I was driving through the neighborhood here once in that Mercedes, and someone threw a can out his car. It landed, smack, on my windshield. I coulda been killed. I drove him off the road. It was a Moroccan. He began swearing. And I said, 'Listen, friend. I'm not Belgian. I'm an Albanian from Kosovo. Do not fight with me, or I burn your house with all your family inside.' Then he backed down. Wanted to know if I was Muslim. Ha! I didn't wanna stay in Belgium. I can't accept my daughter marrying a Negro or a Pakistani or a Turk. And that'll happen, because love knows no color. The first time I was with my wife she called me the next morning and I said, 'I don't wanna go any further with you because you're Slovak and I want to marry Albanian.' But my wife insisted. 'Please, Anton, I want to see you.' And now I'm married to a Slovak woman. If only Belgians lived here, okay, then maybe I would have stayed. Here is nice, but home is home."

In the meantime, things had gotten totally out of hand in Kosovo. With the advent of the Kosovo Liberation Army, the lingering conflict between the Albanian majority and the Serbian minority had turned into outright war. At the beginning of 1998, the situation was worsening by the day. In Antwerp, Anton watched it all on TV. "My people were being wiped out. Albanians from all over the world were returning to Kosovo to fight for independence, and I should stay here? No, I reported to the Kosovo Liberation Army as an instructor. I taught the soldiers self-defense. They didn't know anything. I taught them how to hold a machine gun, how to wring somebody's neck.

"I got in my—your—Mercedes 190 and drove to Kosovo."

THIRST

*B*ang. And again: *BANG!*

Rocks the size of cobblestones ricochet against Amadou's protective plate. But I don't have time to worry about the Mercedes. I have to concentrate on my driving. Sidi Ali and I have left the blacktop of the Trans-Sahara Highway and are driving now on a piste, a road consisting of nothing more than tire tracks in the sand. Finally—finally—I'm in the middle of the bare, barren desert. I jolt to and fro; the car swerves left and right. At times, I feel the wheels skid, but if I give it enough gas, I keep moving. It feels like I'm slipping on an icy sidewalk instead of driving over a white-hot sandy plain.

It's not just the concentration that dispels my fear; it's the fun I'm having as well. I tear through the sand, jerking the steering wheel just like that seedy Frenchman at the campground in Dakhla.

Yee-ha! Motocross heaven.

The Mercedes throws up an enormous cloud of dust. The window's open, and my hair is full of sand. The stereo's belting out some music. I bum a cigarette from Sidi Ali.

This is WILD!

I finally understand the thrill of desert driving.

Thanks to the Trans-Sahara Highway, all the trans-Sahara traffic passes through Mauritania these days. That wasn't always the case. Until the mid-1990s, everyone drove through Algeria. That was true even for the Sahara's first motorist, the Belgian baron Pierre de Grawhez, an avid race-car driver who would win many a race in his life. He, his brother, and a small group of other young Belgian barons disembarked in Algiers with four automobiles in early January 1901. A month and a half later they reached the small oasis town of Ghardaïa, 375 miles south—still far from the heart of the Sahara but a start. Considering the challenge, the trip went rather well. Only two cars had to quit, because . . . they got stuck in the sand too often. The reason: too little ground clearance. Indeed, little has changed since then.

The Belgian nobles soon had imitators. Henri de Rothschild, a French baron—driving was still a decidedly elite pastime at the dawn of the twentieth century—left for Algeria with two Mercedes touring cars in 1905. Later, in the magazine *La vie au grand air* (Life in the Open Air), he published the first automobile guide to the Sahara—a forerunner of *Sahara Overland*, you might say. He complains a lot in that article, especially about getting stuck in the sand so often. In an illustration accompanying the piece, we see someone—the baron, or more likely his chauffeur—kneeling in the sand. He's trying to free the dug-in wheels with a shovel— that hasn't changed in a hundred years, either. The Mercs, by the way, performed superbly, and after a few weeks of motocrossing De Rothschild returned to France safe and sound.

Adventurous drivers journeyed ever deeper into the desert.

The French tried it primarily in Algeria; the English, in Libya, the Sudan, and Egypt. Nonetheless, it wasn't till 1922 that the Sahara in its entirety was traversed by car, an honor reserved for a team in service to the automaker André Citroën.

In twenty days, Georges-Marie Haardt and Louis Audouin-Dubreuil led an expedition of five cars from Touggourt, a little more than three hundred miles south of Algiers, all the way to Timbuktu in present-day Mali. You'd think there'd be countless sensational stories to tell about that trip—tales of the members of the expedition suffering terrible thirst, for instance, or engaging the natives in gunfights. But nothing of the sort occurred. Apart from a few minor repairs and near accidents (one of the expedition leaders fell asleep at the wheel), everything went according to plan. Did Haardt and Audouin-Dubreuil excel at avoiding disaster, then? Was Citroën perhaps the world's best automaker that his five cars returned from the challenge without so much as a scratch? You'd almost think so. (By comparison, more than half the participants in today's Paris–Dakar Rally, which takes place in that same Sahara, usually drop out.)

The car Citroën chose to conquer the Sahara was the Autochenille, a car that looked like a half-track. It was, in fact, a cross between an ordinary Citroën and a Caterpillar-type vehicle. The Autochenille was a forerunner of our four-wheel drive. You could take it on all sorts of terrain: muddy mountain slopes, snowy plains, and sandy deserts. That, at least, was the idea. André Citroën had devised this first trans-Sahara trip by automobile in order to demonstrate the car's versatility. It soon became apparent, however, that the vehicle was far from ideal for the desert tour. The biggest problem: the Autochenille was a gas-guzzler. Gas depots had to be constructed all along the route to permit the cars to complete the tour. And in reality Citroën had little confidence in the vehicle's publicly praised all-terrain characteristics, for the route had to be leveled as well. While French soldiers looked on, the native inhabitants of the rockiest areas were forced to build a piste for the expedition. The tour was totally under the supervision of the French army so that even the chance of attacks from Tuareg rebels could be kept to a minimum. Of course, this was all kept carefully out of the papers. The first trans-Sahara trip was no old-fashioned adventure full of danger and uncertainty but a modern, thoroughly prepared publicity stunt in which nothing was allowed to go wrong.

In the long run, in any event, the tour brought Citroën little success in North Africa—you never see a Citroën here.

The route the Citroën expedition followed remained the most popular among Sahara travelers for decades thereafter. It wasn't until the mid-1990s that bandits, terrorists, and Tuareg rebels put an end to that. As recently as 2003, a group of thirty-two Western European tourists was kidnapped in the Algerian Sahara and only released months later. Nowadays, hardly any Europeans drive through Algeria, and the so-called Atlantic Route, the route I'm following at the moment, is the only safe and practical one to take to West Africa.

The Atlantic Route has gotten much easier to travel the last few years. Since Morocco subdued Polisario, you no longer have to cross Western Sahara in a military convoy, and the approaching completion of the Trans-Sahara Highway is making it easier still. But as a result, for many experienced desert drivers the fun appears to have gone out of it. As they complain, anyone can cross the desert now. Consequently, crossing the desert is assuming major proportions. You already had the Paris–Dakar Rally, but lately rallies, "challenges," and races have been organized for ordinary cars as well. It began a few years ago in Britain with Plymouth–Dakar, a tour anyone could join as long as he bought his car for less than a hundred pounds (about $160) and donated it on arrival in Africa to be auctioned off for a good cause. Plymouth–Dakar is a lively affair, more traveling house party than survival tour, and it quickly drew imitators. Now you have Amsterdam–Dakar, Switzerland–Dakar, Budapest–Bamako. It seems like there's an alternative Dakar Rally for every capital in Europe.

It may appear as if all danger has passed, but for the time being, the trip to Dakar still provides peril and trouble enough. For starters, for your car. The loose sand I'm driving on soon gives way to a rock-hard washboard piste. It feels exactly as the name suggests: it's as if you were driving over an old-fashioned washboard. A piste like this consists of countless alternating furrows and ridges at right angles to the direction of the trail. Call it a corrugated sheet of sand. Sometimes, the washboard is no longer than a few hundred yards; more often, it continues for miles. Sometimes, the ridges are a half inch high; sometimes, nearly four inches. Driving over them, you feel your car is about to burst at the joints. Everything shakes and jolts. Instead of a responsive steering wheel, you feel like you're holding a jackhammer.

There are two ways to drive over a washboard piste. Either very, very slowly, about the speed of a bicycle, or so fast the car's wheels just barely touch the top of the ridges. That's dangerous, because you hover like an airplane that can't quite take off. But whatever you do, your car takes such a pounding that sooner or later something breaks.

"I had to make a crash landing in the Sahara Desert six years ago. Something in my plane's engine had broken, and since I had neither a mechanic nor passengers in the plane with me, I was preparing to undertake the difficult repair job by myself. For me it was a matter of life or death: I had only enough drinking water for eight days. The first night, then, I went to sleep on the sand a thousand miles from any inhabited country. I was more isolated than a man shipwrecked on a raft in the middle of the ocean."

The passage comes from Antoine de Saint-Exupéry's classic novella *The Little Prince*. Although it's an airplane that's broken down, I figure that the mixture of dread, determination, and a glimmer of hope that speaks through here applies to car trouble in the desert as well. It is, in any case, my greatest fear: that something in my car will fail.

No, it's not car trouble; it's what comes after that that I'm afraid of.

On account of the combination of high temperature and dry air, a person loses fluid at an alarming rate in the Sahara. If you sit in the full sun—and remain perfectly motionless—at a temperature of a hundred degrees, you lose more than a quart of water an hour. In five hours, you're seriously dehydrated; in two days, dead. *Sahara Overland* recommends drinking more than five quarts of water a day in the winter and more than two and a half gallons in the summer. If you don't keep to that, things go wrong fast.

The average adult human body consists of more than thirteen gallons of water. There are nasty consequences to the loss of even a small percentage of that, let alone what happens when you're seriously dehydrated. It begins with innocent symptoms like dry lips, loss of appetite, and headache. But after that, with a fluid loss of about 10 percent, the symptoms rapidly progress to dizziness, trouble breathing, sunken eyes, a lack of saliva, and a tendency to babble. At that point, you can still stem the tide by getting out of the sun and especially by drinking lots of water. It's another matter when serious dehydration sets in. With a loss of 20 percent of body fluid, or some two and a half gallons, there's no chance of survival without admission to the hospital: the tongue and throat are so swollen that you can no longer drink on your own. You go deaf, your lips turn blue, your skin shrivels up and loses feeling. The body manufactures large quantities of endorphins, which produce a sense of euphoria. Finally, delirium sets in—as with the character Captain Haddock in the classic Tintin comic book *The Crab with the Golden Claws*, who, stranded in the Sahara, mistakes Tintin for a bottle of champagne and wants to "uncork" him. During the terminal phase of dehydration, the body extracts so much fluid from the blood that the blood thickens and the body's heat can no longer be released through the skin. The body temperature rises dramatically, one or more of the vital organs (the heart, brain, and lungs) fail, and death follows.

BANG! Another rock hits the protective plate.

HENNNGGGGGGGGGG. The Mercedes shakes and jolts on the washboard. Then, suddenly, a patch of loose sand. I space out for a second and quickly feel the car getting stuck.

Plop.

The engine dies. I get out and survey the damage. It's not as bad as I feared; the wheels haven't sunk very deep in the sand.

"We'll be outta that in no time," I tell Sidi Ali.

He nods . . . and goes and sits on a pile of sand while I begin to dig.

"Can't ya lend me a hand?" I ask him, annoyed.

" 'Snot my fault, is it?" he answers, pulling his baseball cap low over his eyes.

Fifteen minutes of digging, sand ladders under the wheels, start the car, and the job is finished. But in the meantime the clinical descriptions of the symptoms of dehydration in the Sahara have taken on a personal meaning. I have parched lips, a dry mouth, and black spots in front of my eyes. I have to hold on to the car to avoid falling over. Sidi Ali is watching me closely, but when I glance at him, he quickly looks away. My whole body is screaming, WATER! And that's after only fifteen minutes of exertion in the full sun.

Hundreds of people die of thirst in the Sahara every year. Most are West Africans who want to try their luck in Europe. We rarely hear anything about them. At most, there might be a tiny item in the paper if a lot have perished at once. It's another matter if Western tourists vanish in the desert.

I still remember two Dutch youths, Peter Teggelaar and Marc Gilsing, getting lost in the Algerian Sahara in the summer of 1993. Their disappearance dominated the news in the Netherlands for weeks; their photos appeared on the front page of the country's largest paper. They were healthy young Dutch boys: Marc with neat, combed-back hair, a broad grin, and wide-set eyes; Peter, longish, shaggy red locks, a somewhat pockmarked face, pinched eyes, more serious looking. I recognized myself in them. I was the same age and identified totally with their thirst for adventure. For that's what they were, adventurers. But not irresponsible. Their only—and fatal—mistake was being too trusting.

Peter and Marc had had the same plan as I do now: to drive an old car through the Sahara and sell it at a profit in West Africa. They'd taken off well prepared. The car, a Peugeot 505, was in good order. They had spare parts, flares, a compass, and a fire extinguisher with them. Peter had even taken a course in car repair. They'd chosen the Algerian route. Everything had gone smoothly until Tamanrasset in southern Algeria. There, at the end of July, for $250, they had hired a guide to take them to Niger.

And then weeks went by without the two getting in touch with their parents. The alarm was sounded. Friends distributed "missing" posters in southern Algeria. "You prepare yourself for the worst, of course," Peter's father told a reporter, "but Peter and Marc are guys who always land on their feet." The "missing" posters had an adverse effect. Peter and Marc were said to have been spotted in a hotel in Nigeria, hundreds of miles farther south. They were reported to have been murdered in the Algerian desert town of In Guezzam. Those were all rumors.

The guide turned out to be a fraud. He lost his way not long after they left Tamanrasset. Whenever he got behind the wheel, he wound up stuck in the sand. He cracked the radiator against a rock. Peter managed to fix that for the time being, but the guide was such a reckless driver that a little later he damaged a wheel so badly that they couldn't go any farther. In hopes of being spotted by passersby, they pushed the car up a hill. At night, they sent up flares. Finally, they even set their car on fire. But no one noticed them. They had no idea where they were. They waited seven days for help, sharing their water with the bastard who'd gotten them into this mess. On the eighth day, the guide left on foot. Peter and Marc stayed by the car.

What surprised me, and what I admired about them, was that they weren't afraid of dying. "They were mainly concerned not for their own fate but for the grief they'd caused others," Peter's father told the press. He'd gathered that from their diary, in which they also tried to arrange their estates, dividing their furniture among their family and pals and asking their parents to care for their girl-friends. A month after their disappearance, the Algerian army finally organized a large-scale search party. Their remains were found about a hundred miles south of Tamanrasset.

No rock cracks my oil pan or radiator. My Mercedes survives the washboard piste. Moreover, the desert driving lasts only a few hours. The next blacktop portion of the Trans-Sahara Highway has already appeared on the horizon. In the end, the only similarity between my journey and the disastrous trip of Peter and Marc is the guide. Mine, too, is a fraud.

Sidi Ali, who has actually kept his mouth shut and his hands off my CD player since we got stuck in the sand, gestures for me to stop.

There beside the highway is a wooden shed. I hear the drone of a diesel generator.

"We're gonna sleep here tonight," he says.

Now what, I think. "But we agreed you'd take me to a nice spot," I stammer. "You talked about sand dunes, about sleeping among the camels."

Sidi Ali looks at me with raised eyebrows.

"But it *is* nice here."

We're in the world's most beautiful desert, and my guide expects me to sleep beside the highway in a cloud of diesel fumes.

I explode with rage.

I walk around the car, kick a few stones, and fling Dutch obscenities in Sidi's direction. He stares at me like a frightened dog.

"Fine, you can stay here," I say after a long silence. "I'll drive a little farther and look for a nice place myself." I must and will have my Saint-Exupéry night in the desert under the starry sky. Sidi Ali thinks that's a bad plan. Naturally, he's afraid I'll leave him behind. And rightly. But despite his objections, I do as I please. A sand path leads away from the Trans-Sahara Highway a few miles farther on. I see an idyllic little spot in the distance: a few low sand dunes, a crooked acacia tree, even camel tracks. I pitch my tent here. I make a cup of soup. I lie down for a while.

I fall asleep before sundown and dream of stars.

The author's Mercedes in front of his apartment building in Amsterdam.

All photographs by Jeroen van Bergeijk, except where noted.

The Grande Africa, *from Palermo, moored in the port of Amsterdam. Dozens of such ships, loaded with used cars, leave Western Europe for West Africa each month. The* Grande Africa *can make the trip in three weeks. Driving takes three months.*

From Zagora, Morocco, to Timbuktu is fifty-two days by camel. But almost no one goes by camel anymore. Even nomads drive Benzes.

The entrance to Tan-Tan, a little town in southern Morocco.

Mauritanian mechanics mount a plate under the author's Mercedes to protect its oil pan from desert rocks.

Sidi Ali, the young Moor who served as the author's guide through the Mauritanian desert.

The Trans-Sahara Highway.

The end of the road, some 120 kilometers (seventy-five miles) from the Mauritanian capital of Nouakchott.

A camel crossing the Trans-Sahara Highway near Nouakchott.

A victim of Nouakchott's free-for-all traffic.

The ferry between Mauritania and Senegal. The passengers are Senegalese headed home to celebrate Tabaski, the Muslim Festival of Sacrifice. The sheep in the trunk will be part of the slaughter.

Senegal's main east–west road hasn't been repaved in years.

Baobab trees, which can live for centuries, dot the West African savanna.

"Every now and then a herd of longhorned cattle crossed the road. The road led through villages with mud huts where children went to school under a tree and where, if you stopped, you were offered a bowl of fresh water drawn from a well in a bucket. They hardly spoke French here, and a white man was still a curiosity."

A mechanic in Bamako, Mali, replaces the struts on the author's Mercedes, broken by driving over an unpaved desert road so rough it resembled a washboard.

The road to Kumasi, Ghana.

A parts store in Suame Magazine, the largest auto repair center in all of West Africa.

"A Benin car market reminds you of a prison yard. It's an enormous walled parking lot. The walls are topped with barbed wire, and every fifty feet is a thirteen-foot-tall watchtower made of used lumber and corrugated metal roofing. The car dealers man their towers like prison guards, looking out over their cars and their customers."

This taxi in Benin gives "filled to capacity" a whole new meaning.

The end of the trip getting near: only 139 kilometers (85 miles) to go to Ouagadougou, the capital of Burkina Faso.

Sold! The new owner with the author's trusted Mercedes 190.

Proceeds from the sale.

HEART OF DARKNESS

Nouakchott, the capital of Mauritania, is a city with no cinemas, department stores, theaters, bookshops, discos, concert halls, or bars. Everything that makes a city fun is missing here. Everything that makes a city unpleasant—people, cars, filth—can be found here in spades. Nouakchott is like a cream pie without the whipped cream: a piece of dry crust you can barely stand to swallow. It's like the cabs that drive around here: an unpainted wreck in which the only things that still work are the ones it absolutely, positively cannot do without.

The entrance to the city is a garbage dump. Coming from the north, you drive for miles through an apocalyptic landscape of piles of stinking refuse, smoldering fires, flapping plastic bags, and the rusting hulks of junked cars.

A few highways are paved, but most of the "streets" are sandy trails where your car gets stuck just as bad as in the barren, lifeless desert. In fact, it *is* desert here. Not counting cities on the edge of the desert like Cairo, Nouakchott is the Sahara's largest metropolis. In 1963 it was a sleepy little fishing village. But after the country gained its independence from France, there had to be a capital. Nouakchott was designed for fifteen thousand people; nearly a million live here now.

Still, Nouakchott does *try* to be a capital. There's a TV station, a stadium, a presidential palace—and a museum. The Musée National is the only museum in Mauritania. It takes fifteen minutes to find somebody who can sell me a ticket. The building consists of two galleries. One contains a collection of potsherds and arrowheads; the other is devoted to the local costume. I'm the only visitor. By the time I'm ready to leave, the only guard has laid out some merchandise on a bench by the exit as a makeshift museum store: a T-shirt, a few bracelets, some books, and some folders. Included is a brochure praising the investment climate in Mauritania. "Special Advertisement Section to *The New York Times*," it says in big letters on the front. I start to stick the thing in my bag, but the guard stops me. It costs ten dollars. Pay for an advertising pamphlet? Indignant, I'd like to give the guard a lecture: If you want people to invest in your country . . . Oh, never mind. Maybe he's right: he can tell from my appearance—scruffy beard, dirty clothes—that *I* won't be making any investments. I toss the pamphlet back.

Nouakchott is hit by sandstorms two hundred days a year. There's one raging right now. This storm—it's more like a sand *fog*—will last a week. If you want to go out in such a storm, you better make sure your whole body is covered. The sand gets in everything: in your bag, in your food, even in your underwear. But a storm like this has more consequences than just physical discomfort. For one thing, you can't drive your car in a sandstorm. Not so much because of the poor visibility, as because your car is literally sandblasted. The finish dulls; the windshield and headlight glass turns matte. The glass in some Mauritanian cars has turned almost milky white.

A country's traffic is a metaphor for its culture. In the Netherlands, the cars gleam, the roads are well maintained, and rules and warnings ("If you can read this, YOU'RE TOO CLOSE!") encourage motorists to drive safely and courteously. At the same time, if there are no cops in sight, everyone drives over the speed limit. The Dutchman likes to think of his country that way: clean and orderly but with a touch of antiauthoritarianism.

In Mauritania, the drivers fear neither God nor man. In the week I'm here, I see a collision per day. The traffic in Nouakchott is a disorderly mess, a jumble, a free-for-all in which everyone does whatever he wants. The cars here—the overwhelming majority of which are Benzes, by the way—are like the bicycles Dutch students ride: rusty wrecks with no lights. In the West, these cars couldn't even be sold for parts: everything of value has already been removed. Brakes, headlights, the upholstery on the seats, let alone chrome mirrors or a working CD player—everything is missing. But still, it's not the condition of the Mauritanian auto fleet that makes you suspect that driving here offers a worse chance of survival than a game of Russian roulette. It's what Mauritanians do with their moving wrecks. Cars have to share the road with donkey and horse carts. Those just *have* to be passed, even if it's not possible. And so people always pass on the shoulder or over the median strip. No one waits for the stoplight (there are only three stoplights in all of Nouakchott anyhow), and everyone drives into oncoming traffic. Rules concerning the right-of-way do not exist. No, that's not true; the rule is, whoever's the most aggressive has the right-of-way.

The longer I stay in Nouakchott, the more I hate the town. A city with no culture or diversion, where you can't see any farther than twenty yards during the sandstorms, where people drive as if they were driving bumper cars at an amusement park—I don't understand how anyone could enjoy living here.

Like Alexander Dewilde from Belgium.

Alexander is young, clever, and enterprising. The very things that annoy me about Nouakchott appeal to him. The things I miss leave him cold. Alexander is a former trader in used cars. After years of driving cars here from Belgium, he sold refrigerators for a while. Then he bought a restaurant, Café Restau Bruxelles, which stands on the edge of town where the Trans-Sahara Highway begins. In a country where the only coffee is instant and the only orange juice comes in a carton, Alexander serves real espresso and fresh-squeezed OJ. Croissants and camel sandwiches with mayonnaise are also on the menu. But unfortunately, no Flemish specialties like mussels or fries. "They don't like that stuff here."

Alexander decided to settle here for good in 2000. He became a Muslim and speaks fluent Hassānīya, the local Arabic dialect. Because Mauritanians are night people, his business doesn't start jumping until around midnight. He has to be at the market to do his shopping the next morning at six, and a couple of hours later his restaurant is open again already for breakfast. Consequently, he hasn't had a good night's rest in a year. "I don't get much sleep. Nights a little, mornings a little," he says, then asks anxiously, "I look it, don't I?" I don't dare tell him the truth. He does indeed have bags under his eyes. Alexander is twenty-eight, but I'd take him for ten years older.

"I work like a madman. I don't have any days off or vacation," Alexander says. "Life is much harder here than in Belgium." But you won't hear Alexander complain. He feels that other things compensate for the harshness of life in Mauritania. "Life is much more simple and straightforward here. I don't feel at home in Europe anymore. Too many rules. You need a diploma for everything. It's too much for me. The things *you* miss here—movies, cafés, concerts—those mean nothing to me. For me, life is very simple.

I'm easily satisfied. Work, make a little money, eat, drink, sleep. That's about it. I try to be a good Muslim. But the main reason I like it here is that I feel free here. Yes, free. Let me give you an example. I don't have a mailbox. I love it! In Belgium they stuff that thing full, you know. With bills and letters. But they don't exist here, mailboxes. I find that liberating."

Alexander may work hard; his Moorish clientele certainly does not. "A Moor looks down on physical labor," says Alexander. Mauritania is a segregated society: Moors and blacks live in separate worlds. Slavery was only officially abolished here in 1981. In practice, little has changed since then: the Moorish minority still calls the shots, and blacks do the dirty work. I had noticed that already in the mechanic Amadou's workplace in Nouadhibou, and I notice it again now in Alexander's kitchen, where only blacks are behind the counter. But if black people do all the work, what do the Moors do?

"All a Moor cares about," says Alexander, "is *chep-chep*."

Chep-chep is something like finagling. *Chep-chep* means trying to gain an advantage from everything. *Chep-chep* means doing business with a wink and a nod. *Chep-chep* means playing a game where dirty tricks are allowed. *Chep-chep* means reading between the lines. *Chep-chep* drives the rigid Dutch Calvinist in me crazy. But not Alexander, who deals with nothing else all day long.

Chep-chep, Alexander explains, is the orange vendor who sticks a few rotten oranges in your order when you're not looking.

Chep-chep is the plumber who comes to fix Alexander's broken toilet but manages to "repair" it in such a way that it breaks again in two weeks and Alexander has to call him again.

Chep-chep is the free meals Alexander gives to influential Moors with whom he has to remain on good terms.

But *chep-chep* is especially the trade in used cars.

At the end of the 1990s Alexander could take the cars he bought in Belgium and sell them in Mauritania for three to four times as much. It was a gold mine, and for years he did nothing but commute between Belgium and West Africa with Peugeots and Benzes. He was constantly on the road. In his top year he made the trip no fewer than fourteen times. Occasionally, Alexander would place an ad in a Belgian newspaper: "Wanted: Adventurous types for trip to Africa," that sort of thing. If people called, Alexander would quickly buy a bunch of cars and minivans, set out with the participants in a caravan, and then pay for their plane tickets home. A cheap vacation for them, profit for him. *Chep-chep*.

He crammed those vehicles full of junk he found on the street: old refrigerators, chairs, tables, steam irons, anything that was still useful. Then he would sell the stuff in Morocco to defray his costs. *Chep-chep*.

There wasn't yet any Trans-Sahara Highway then; you still had to drive through the sand and on the last stretch even over the Atlantic Ocean beach. So as not to get lost in the desert, Alexander would always hire a guide to lead him to Nouakchott. But those guides would sometimes intentionally lead Alexander through heavy terrain in hopes his car would give out. Once, Alexander got a hole in the oil pan of his Peugeot 405 and his engine froze up. And once he lost a Mercedes van to the rising tide. Those stranded autos disappeared within a day, stolen by the dishonest guides. *Chep-chep*.

Although Alexander often sold his cars in Nouakchott, he sometimes continued on to Senegal or Mali. There he picked up masks and ornaments that he would sell during the summer at outdoor music festivals in Europe. *Chep-chep*.

In the beginning it was fun driving cars to Africa, but once you'd done it a few times, the fun wore off. So Alexander tried something more ambitious: he began importing cars by ship. The good news was that he could import many more cars at a time; the bad news, that he had to pay import duties. Until then, he'd been able to avoid that by slipping the customs agents at the border something. But that wasn't possible at the port—there was hardly any *chep-chep* there. You had to pay the full amount; otherwise, you didn't get your cars. But Alexander eventually thought of something for that, too. He shipped his cars not to Nouakchott but to Dakar in neighboring Senegal. There he arranged transit documents for Morocco. Of course, the cars never arrived in Morocco. They were disposed of on the way, in Mauritania. *Chep-chep*.

In 2001 the business collapsed. Large, professional dealers had discovered there was money to be made in the African car trade. The market in Mauritania was flooded, prices plummeted, there was hardly anything to be made anymore. So long, *chep-chep*.

The heyday of the used-car trade in Nouakchott may be over, but that doesn't mean there aren't any car traders left. At the Auberge Sahara, a popular gathering spot for travelers driving across Africa in their own cars, they're as thick as fleas.

A mousy man who can't stop looking around nervously is sitting at the communal table. He has the same bulging eyes as the actor Peter Lorre. His name is Thomas, he's from Denmark, and he's been staying at the Auberge Sahara for a couple of weeks. As soon as he notices that I speak English, he comes over to have a chat. "I wanna get out of here," he confides after a while, speaking with a lisp. "I hate it here." He knows only a few words of French, and even those make for confusion. " 'Milk,' that's *lait*, right?" he asks. He pronounces the word as "lut." I nod in agreement. "Nobody here understands what I say."

Thomas sniffles and coughs. It's over ninety degrees, but he's wearing a sweater and has a wool scarf wrapped around his neck. Thomas is sick. Chronically sick. Something with his lungs. He's on disability in Denmark and has been using the money from that for almost a year to travel to warm climates. That's what the doctor recommended. Thomas lived in Spain for half a year, then in Morocco. He thought the dry desert air would do him good, but he hadn't reckoned with the sandstorms. His lungs can't stand the dust in the air.

And now he wants to return to Denmark. But it's not that simple. The problem is he's almost out of money: it never occurred to him that the banks and cash machines in Mauritania might not accept Danish credit cards. And so he's decided to become a car trader in spite of himself: for a week now he's been trying to unload his twenty-year-old Audi. But there's no demand at all for Audis in Mauritania, old or new. "The best offer I've had was five hundred dollars," he says indignantly. "Yeah, come on. I paid fifteen hundred for it in Denmark." And now he no longer knows what to do. The sandstorms are driving him crazy, but selling his car for five hundred bucks . . . He needs more money than that just to buy a ticket home. He simply has to get more money for it. And if he can't, the only alternative is to drive back to Morocco. But he's scared to death his car won't make it. He already had car trouble a couple of times on the way here. One of his shocks gave out, and his exhaust pipe fell off. Next thing you know, he'll be stuck in the middle of the desert—with no money *and* no car.

The twentysomething Frenchman Jean-Pierre is, if possible, even more desperate than Thomas. Jean-Pierre wears his hair in dreadlocks; his jeans look like they haven't been washed in a month. He's trying to sell not only his car (a Renault 5, another model that no one here wants) but his personal possessions as well. He's peddling his cell phone, his camera, and his watch. He even wants to sell the carpet he bought as a souvenir of Morocco. It's obvious to everyone that he's hard up, and naturally that weakens his bargaining position. The owner of the Auberge Sahara offers him fifteen dollars for the carpet; one of the hotel's guests is willing to take the phone off his hands for ten. One afternoon I see him hawking his stuff among the tables outside Snack Iraq, a *shawarma*, or gyro, joint where a lot of Mauritanian car traders do business. He accosts every customer and is treated with the same contempt as the black street vendors. One man asks to see all his wares. He even has the Frenchman unroll his Moroccan carpet, only to wave him away again with a flick of his hand. Jean-Pierre slinks off with his tail between his legs.

And then there are the three Germans: weak, pudgy, middle-aged men with drooping mustaches and vests with lots of pockets. They're noisy, drink lots of beer, and unlike Jean-Pierre and Thomas know exactly what they're doing. They all drive Mercedes and have been dealing cars in West Africa for years. But they don't want to talk about it. "Sure, I'm gonna tell you everything," one of them says. "I'd have to be out of my mind." He will, however, say one thing. "You're not too bright if you sell here. You have to go to Mali. You'll get a lot more there."

"Ah, into the heart of darkness," whispers Simon.

His eyes sparkle. A slight grin plays around his mouth.

We're standing in front of a yellowed Michelin map of West Africa pinned to the wall in a hallway of the Auberge Sahara. I look at this map every day, pondering how to continue my trip. Simon has just asked me what my plans are, and I've pointed to the border town of Rosso. Rosso lies on the Senegal, a mighty big river, resembling an immense snake uncoiled, with its head in the sea, its body at rest on the border between Mauritania and Senegal, and its tail lost in the depths of Mali.

"That's where I wanna cross," I tell him.

I like Simon. He's funny. He's well-read. Simon is on his way to South Africa on his motorcycle. I wonder if he'll ever get there. The first time he had to ride off road, in the sand between Nouadhibou and Nouakchott, he fell off his bike. A couple of passing tourists took him to the hospital in Nouakchott. The damage: a few ugly bruises and a broken collarbone. That was two months ago. Simon has been waiting for the doctors to say it's okay for him to travel again. I admire him for not returning to London. That was the obvious thing to do: recuperate at home and continue his trip later. But Simon was afraid that if he waited too long, he'd never complete the journey, and he dreaded facing his friends, too: barely begun and already a failure. He started talking about it yesterday after a couple of shots of whiskey—Jean-Pierre had traded his camera for a bottle of Johnnie Walker and treated everyone. Simon's ashamed, and every time a biker arrives at the Auberge Sahara full of enthusiastic tales about riding in the desert, he confronts that shame anew. He's bored to death in Nouakchott. So last week—to hell with the doctors—he went for a little ride, a weekend trip to Saint-Louis, Senegal, about 190 miles south. He crossed the border at Rosso.

"And? What was it like there?" I ask impatiently. "Was it really so bad?"

"I don't wanna spoil your fun," says Simon. "You'll have to experience it for yourself. But I can tell you this much: take plenty of cash."

Rosso is known as the most notorious border crossing in West Africa, some say in all of Africa. The border is supposedly occupied not only by a small army of corrupt customs agents but also by dozens of hustlers who try every trick in the book to rob travelers blind. Stories of swindles that seem to happen there as if they were the most normal thing in the world circulate on the Internet. The message: whatever you do, avoid Rosso.

The most notorious border crossing in Africa? I've got to see that. The heart of darkness? Bring it on.

A few days later I sit in my car, my knees knocking, outside the compound that houses the customs headquarters in Rosso. There's a big iron gate at the entrance to bar "outsiders," and everyone here is an outsider unless they manage to convince the gatekeeper that they really want to cross the border. But before I can give that man some money, I'm accosted by another, uniformed man. He wants to see my papers. Five or six other men are crowded around him.

"Can't I come in first?" I ask the man in uniform.

"Passport and driver's license," he orders again.

"Give him the papers!" shouts one of the bystanders.

"Hey, I'll help you!" cries another.

"Where are you from?" a third demands.

What now? I would like to get inside first, but there doesn't appear to be much room for discussion. And what possible harm could it do to show my papers? I've already done that countless times the past few weeks. There's a police post every dozen miles in Africa where bored officials want to check your passport. Sometimes they write your name in a big book, one of those books you know no one will ever open again once it's full.

So I take out my passport and license, and before I know it, the man in the uniform has snatched them out of my hands. Instead of checking them, he passes them on to two of the bystanders. A man with a pair of 1980s Madonna sunglasses and a harelip gets my passport; an adolescent with a Michael Jordan basketball shirt, my driver's license. Both immediately take off.

Shit, this isn't going well.

What now? Which one should I follow? Should I save my license or my passport? Meanwhile, other cars are waiting, honking their horns, and the man in the uniform—What is he actually? A soldier? A customs agent?—has walked on again. The bystanders shout that I should drive on. One pounds on the roof; another knocks on the window and makes gestures I don't understand.

Then the gate of the compound swings open. I drive in and join a line of cars. The men with my papers are already waiting for me. Phew, what a relief! You meet hustlers like these two at every border crossing in Africa. The African hustler wants to help you cut through the red tape. He shows you which rooms, cubicles, and offices you have to go to and in what order. He tells you what you have to pay and to whom. Most Westerners don't care for hustlers. They find their services superfluous (which they usually are) and don't trust their information (with good reason). But it's my experience that a hustler is usually well worth the money. Not because he knows the way through the African bureaucracy so well, but because he keeps other hustlers at bay. If you don't have a hustler, others will keep bothering you. Once you've hired one, the rest slink away.

So I let myself be taken in tow by the two who have my papers. The one with the harelip is named Abdul; his younger colleague is Alex. We walk from one cubicle to the next, we enter rooms, we walk upstairs and stand in line. Abdul and Alex tell me what I have to pay. A few dollars here, a few dollars there. I don't know what I'm paying for. I don't know whom I'm paying. But the collection of stamps, official-looking receipts, and documents grows and grows. Until Abdul declares our journey at an end. Now the only thing left is to get on the boat.

That's easier said than done. The day after tomorrow is the Festival of Sacrifice, and the ferry is crowded. Thousands of Senegalese who live in Mauritania are headed home. The Festival of Sacrifice—or Tabaski, as it's known here—is one of the most important holidays in Islam. During Tabaski, everyone who can afford to slaughters a sheep. The local newspapers carry alarming reports of a shortage of sheep this year; editorials speak of a scandal involving large sheep traders accused of driving up prices. Ahead of me in line is a Mercedes with a sheep hanging out of the trunk. The gurgling, rattle-like noise issuing from the animal's throat tells me its struggle with death has already begun.

Rosso is the most important border crossing between Mauritania and Senegal, and the ferry, which is supposed to transport all the motorized traffic between the two countries across the river, has room for eight cars or two trucks, tops. The cars and trucks are racing their engines long before the boat docks. Then comes the moment when the first cars are allowed on board, and everyone seems to step on the gas at the same time. The car to my left is up against my mirror; I nudge the car in front of me. It's bumper-to-bumper, door-to-door. Then the boat is full; I've moved about fifteen feet. Another forty-five minutes' wait for the boat to sail over and back.

Senegalese without a car have no problem getting across. Big canoes called pirogues sail back and forth. People, sheep, bags of rice—the boats are so full the water almost runs over the side.

Abdul goes off with fifteen bucks to try to bribe the man who decides who gets on the boat and who doesn't and who blows like crazy the whole time on a whistle dangling from a beautiful white cord hung round his neck. I don't know if the bribe does any good, but with patience, a dent, and a few scratches I finally get on the boat. The trip takes no more than fifteen minutes, but I sweat and shake the whole time. It's a wonder we don't capsize. No one has bothered to raise the gangplank on the front of the ferry. Waves wash over the deck. The cars are parked so close together that I'm unable to open either my left- or my right-hand door. If something happens, I'm sunk—both literally and figuratively.

It's the same story on the other side: a few dollars here, a few dollars there. Then we arrive at a counter where ten officials sit stamping passports. "Give him five bucks," says Abdul, pointing at a fat customs agent half-sprawled on a cot in the corner devouring a pan of gravy-covered rice with a spoon. The agent has his sleeves rolled up as if to say: I'm hard at work.

And then suddenly . . . I've had it. I don't feel like paying anymore. My emotions have finally gotten the best of me. Fuck off, I think. I find the customs agent repulsive, with his grease-flecked shirt, his gravy-covered chin, and his little pig eyes. But above all it's the absolute shamelessness of the corruption that's gotten too much for me. I thought bribery happened on the sly: a banknote folded carefully into the passport so no one notices. Not so open and brazen like this free and easy extortion.

The customs agent stands up, puffing and groaning. He grabs my passport and says, "Ten dollars."

"Why?" I ask.

"Do you want to leave here today?"

"Yeah."

"Then it's ten dollars."

I hesitate, wait a few seconds, and then decide no, I'm not giving him a cent. Let's just see what happens.

Well, not much. He glares at Abdul. He shrugs, turns around, and throws my passport on a pile of other passports. The pile of difficult cases, I suspect. That's going to take a while. As I'm doing it, I know I'm making a mistake. Why are you getting excited? A few bucks and you can leave; you don't have to stay in this stinking hole, waiting among the sweating bodies for a stupid little stamp. Sure, corruption is objectionable, but somehow I find it impossible to summon up any moral indignation about it here. Is it really that much different from the American custom of tipping, but applied to a government bureaucracy? In America you leave tips in restaurants, hotels, and cabs. You're not obliged to leave anything, but everyone does. Leave nothing, or too little, and you're given the cold shoulder and can forget about that nice table or fast service. It's the same in Africa with "gifts" for customs agents, cops, or other officials from whom you want something. The difference is one of degree rather than principle.

My experience from other trips to Africa is that corruption generally isn't as bad as you expect. As long as you keep smiling and talking, you usually get past borders and police checkpoints without too many problems and with a full wallet. Sure, everyone is after your money. Sure, everyone is always begging a gift. But if you don't want to give anything, that's okay, too.

Fatty has downed his rice in ten minutes. He grabs my passport from the pile, glances at me with raised eyebrows, laughs, stamps my passport, and wishes me "bon voyage."

"ALL AFRICANS ARE CHEATS"

Until recently, Saint-Louis, Senegal, was the end of the road for Europeans with used cars to sell. Senegal was a great place to sell your car. The prices were good, and, just as important, you could take a nice vacation here. You never have a problem finding a decent hotel or restaurant in Senegal. So many Europeans came here to sell their cars that a whole new cottage industry sprang up. There were wholesalers and other traders who would buy your car and agents who would help you sell it; hotels and campgrounds catered to Europeans with cars to sell.

Little of that remains.

In 2003 the Senegalese government prohibited the importation of automobiles more than five years old. The official reason for the prohibition was that so many junky old cars were entering the country that they constituted a threat to the environment and traffic safety. The real reason, they think in Saint-Louis, was that the government wanted to stamp out the booming car trade, which was happening almost completely without state supervision and thus taxation. The bureaucrats in the capital, Dakar, wanted all imports to come through the port there so that they wouldn't lose a single cent in import duties. However that may be, the used-car market here has totally collapsed since then.

Martin, a Swiss expatriate who owns the hotel-campground Zebrabar about ten miles outside of Saint-Louis, suffers the consequences of that daily. He gets hardly any customers anymore. The Zebrabar is rather isolated, on a peninsula you can reach only by driving over a mudflat at low tide. Public transportation doesn't exist here; the Zebrabar has to make do with travelers who have their own transportation. And there aren't many of those left in Senegal since the five-year rule went into effect. "If this keeps up, I'll have to close the place," Martin complains. "People with cars to sell go directly from Mauritania to Mali these days."

Besides me, the Zebrabar's only other guest is a German named Werner. And you can't really call him a guest; he's graduated to employee, helps Martin with all sorts of odd jobs, and has been staying here half a year. Werner drives a 1967 Mercedes fire engine and can, if necessary, put out a fire. He's been on his way to South Africa the last two years. "I'm in no hurry," he says with a feeling for understatement. Werner is the type of traveler who thinks his way of traveling is the only proper one and who looks down on all other travelers.

"When do you think you'll make it to South Africa?" I ask him.

"What a typical tourist question."

"What draws you to Africa?" I persist.

"The animals, of course. What do you think?"

"Well, the people maybe, the culture," I venture.

"All Africans are cheats," he says. "This is your first time here, isn't it?"

Saint-Louis is getting ready for Tabaski. On the outskirts of town, thousands of sheep driven together in flocks await last-minute buyers. Some of the animals are skin and bones; others, nicely fattened. In the streets of the old city center, the residents of Saint-Louis have gathered with buckets of soapy water to wash their sheep. Approximately five million sheep will have their throats cut in Senegal tomorrow.

Saint-Louis is the former headquarters of colonial French West Africa. All the French possessions in Africa were governed from here. The old city lies on an island that's the same long, narrow shape as Manhattan but a lot smaller; altogether, the old city center covers an area no larger than a few football fields. Though the city retains something of its old colonial splendor—narrow streets, palatial homes, cast-iron balconies—that won't last much longer. It's all on the verge of collapse. Most of the houses were last painted in colonial times.

I've parked my car right behind city hall. As I'm getting in, I hear a voice behind me call, "Hey, hello, come all the way from Holland?"

Broken Dutch with an accent from the province of Limburg. I turn around, surprised. The young man has a beaming smile on his face.

"Nice car," he says. He's seen my license plate. "Hi, I'm Babacar Diallo. Welcome to Saint-Louis."

Babacar Diallo, call him Abba, lived in the southern Dutch city of Maastricht, the capital of Limburg, for a while, I learn when we sit down together for a beer. He worked there for a manufacturer of frozen croquettes. That sucked. Then he got a job in the local hashish bar. That was better. He married a Limburg woman, Carine, and had a child with her. His son is five now, the same age as mine.

"I call him as often as I can," he says with tears in his eyes. "I really miss him."

"I know exactly what you mean," I say, and take another sip of my drink.

Three or four beers later, with a little prodding from me, the story comes out by fits and starts. His wife was vacationing in Saint-Louis when they met. It was love at first sight. Really. She asked him if he wanted to come to the Netherlands. He didn't have to think twice about that. A few months later they were married, and he left for The Land Where It Always Rains, as he used to call Holland. Limburg was definitely not the promised land. It was nothing but work, work, work. And that rain—oh, man, always that rain. You never saw the sun. Okay, sure, sometimes the sun came out, but never for long. And do you know what he suffered from? Stress. In Limburg he constantly suffered from stress, something that had never bothered him in Senegal. In fact, before he went to Holland, he had never even heard of stress. Sure, he made a lot of money, was able to buy nice clothes and a car, but money never mattered to him. Abba wanted to live. Without stress. It wasn't long before things went wrong. He fought with Carine. The problem was she couldn't keep a secret. That woman couldn't even keep her mouth shut about what they did in bed. The things he confided to her at night during or after their lovemaking—his sister- and mother-in-law were privy to them the next day, too. No, he didn't like that one bit. Fortunately, there was weed. As long as he could smoke a joint, things were okay. Then he could kid himself that he was back in Saint-Louis.

And then he had to go along on a vacation to Thailand. But Abba didn't want to go to Thailand at all. Why couldn't they go to Senegal? It was warm there, too, wasn't it? No, they just had to go to Thailand. And you know what? His sister- and brother-in-law came along, too. Not fun. That's when he split. Left everything behind. Everything—his nice new clothes and his car. He went to

Schiphol Airport and bought a ticket for Dakar. Now he's happy. He has no money, no possessions, and has moved back in with his mother. But now he's happy.

"Say, can I borrow some money from you? Twenty bucks or so? Pay you back tomorrow. Really!"

Where have I heard that before?

Okay, he shouldn't have tried that. But still, I fall like a ton of bricks for Babacar Diallo. Is it his friendly eyes? His generous smile? His disarming broken Dutch? Or is it because he treats me like a person, like an equal; that he's interested not in the Western tourist but in Jeroen van Bergeijk? We arrange to see each other again tomorrow. I can meet his mother and come celebrate Tabaski with him. Sounds good.

Abba arrives the next day on a borrowed moped. I hop on back, and we whiz through the streets of Saint-Louis to his mother's house. He goes too fast—much too fast. We nearly flip over when he takes a sandy curve too hard. An iron door off the street leads to an unkempt courtyard. A couple of old tires lie there; a few chickens scratch around. The sheep was slaughtered this morning, and Abba's mother is stirring a big, steaming pot. Abba introduces me as a friend from Holland, but his mother doesn't even deign to shake my hand. Abba's room, which opens onto the yard, is about ten feet square and has no windows. A bare lightbulb hangs from the ceiling; a mattress lies on the floor. Abba offers me some cheap Spanish wine. The stuff is so sour my mouth puckers. Abba doesn't strike me as a man of great principle, so I don't ask if it's okay: drinking wine on Tabaski. We're enjoying a friendly glass of wine when his cousin comes in. Abba produces a bag of pot. To be polite, I take a couple of hits. As they continue smoking, Abba and his cousin begin talking to each other in Wolof, the local language. The pot isn't so great, and as usual I'm getting paranoid. I have the feeling they're talking about me. They giggle a lot. The more Abba drinks and smokes, the worse his Dutch gets, while I'm having more and more trouble forming a coherent sentence in French.

Abba's cousin takes something out of his bag. He starts making a speech. About how it's Tabaski. About how important it is to give. He would like, therefore, to offer me a gift. He hands me a bracelet. It's an open brass loop with a little ball at either end, the Senegalese version of a Bio-Ray bracelet. What am I supposed to do with this?

"I really can't accept that," I say.

Abba's cousin keeps insisting and acts insulted. "You can't refuse a gift during Tabaski. Giving is very important to us."

"Fine, fine," I say, stuffing the bracelet in my pocket.

Abba takes out a bunch of photos and comes and sits next to me. They're snapshots of him in the Netherlands. A picture of the backyard of a Dutch row house. Abba in a lawn chair. A chubby blond woman with acne leans over him. She has a bottle of Heineken in her hand. Abba at an outdoor café in Maastricht. Abba on the Dam Square in Amsterdam. Then suddenly a photo of Abba in the arms of another blond woman, taken in Senegal, judging by the surroundings.

"Who's that?" I ask.

"Oh, some Swedish girl. I forget her name."

I leaf through the photos: one young white woman after another in Abba's tender embraces. Among the photos is a postcard from Berlin. On the front, the Brandenburg Gate; on the back, a handwritten note: "Dear Abba, I hope you get this card. Your phone number doesn't work. Did you get my other cards? In spite of everything, I still love you. Kisses, Angela."

And another. Greetings from Oslo. "Hey, Abba. Would you please call me? I don't like it that you just took off like that. You just don't do that sort of thing. The car was pretty banged up. I took it to the garage. It cost me nearly thirteen hundred dollars to get it fixed. You promised me you would pay for the damage. I've already sent you a couple letters with my bank information. I want you to pay me back! Call me, Petra."

Abba and his cousin are chatting in Wolof again. Then Abba turns to me.

"You got something from him. Now you have to give something in return."

"What? I beg your pardon?"

"At Tabaski it's very important that the one who receives something also gives something in return. Very important. That is our tradition."

"But, but . . . what should I give then?" I stammer.

Why, money, of course. God, have I had it. I feel like such a dope. We haggle over the amount and settle on fifteen dollars, which seems like a lot, but I'm tipsy and stoned and only want one thing: to get back to my hotel. Then Abba says, "You should only give if you really want to, man."

I throw the money at them, the way that customs agent handled my passport yesterday, and stumble from the room. Later, on my way to the hotel, they pass me on Abba's moped, howling with laughter.

"Are you sure you're okay?" my girlfriend asks on the phone.

"Yeah, fine," I say, lying, my voice skipping. "Well . . . um, no."

I figure I've earned some carefree luxury and comfort and hope to find that in Dakar. Twelve miles from the Senegalese capital, the traffic grinds to a halt; I'm stuck in the stifling heat in a line of honking, exhaust-belching cars for the next three hours. Downtown Dakar seems trapped in a time warp. Practically all the buildings date to the 1970s—nothing earlier, nothing later. It's as if the city was built then and hasn't changed since. You feel as if you've landed on the set of some cheap 1970s TV series; only the cybercafes you find on every corner spoil the illusion.

Dakar is busy, full of aggressive hustlers. It is, thank God, no Nouakchott. There are sewers here, and cars stop for stoplights. There are patisseries, expensive restaurants, nice hotels. There is a cinema here and a bookstore where they actually sell something besides the Koran and *Windows 3.1 for Dummies*. I move into a pricey hotel room with a minibar and crisply starched sheets, then ask at the front desk for the most expensive restaurant in town.

"Lagonda," says the receptionist without hesitation. "I'll call a cab for you."

The entrance to the restaurant Lagonda is a cave. Water trickles down the walls. Tropical fish swim languidly in aquariums recessed in the brown lavalike imitation stone. The restrooms look like old-fashioned ship cabins, complete with portholes. The bar is a sawed-in-half speedboat. The walls are hung with photos of fishermen proudly displaying their catch: sharks, swordfish, and tuna. A theme restaurant in Africa?

The decadence continues out the back. A pier runs from the rear of the restaurant directly into the water. White folks lounge on beach chairs, enjoying the setting sun. Senegalese in sailor suits stand ready to take their orders.

I order a cocktail with a little umbrella. I feel like the cartoon character Tintin in the comic book *Tintin in the Congo*.

But however much the proprietors of Lagonda try to keep the real Africa at bay, they don't quite succeed. You can see the adjoining public beach from the pier. A bare-chested man sits on a rock washing his T-shirt. Children in rags poke at the rotting carcass of a fish with a stick. Another man pulls down his pants and takes a dump. With a view like that, carefree contentment is no longer possible. Embarrassed, I pick at my dinner with a silver fork that costs as much as three average Senegalese make in a month. I can't enjoy my food. In the cab back to the hotel, my stomach begins to gurgle. The diarrhea comes a couple hours later, followed by my dinner. I spend the next two days either in bed or on or above the toilet.

Justice? Perhaps, but I still think I've earned a little carefree luxury and comfort. If not in Dakar, in Gambia then. Gambia is an insignificant little country. It's the smallest country in Africa, consisting of a strip of land on either side of the Gambia River. With a total area of 4,363 square miles, it's about a quarter the size of the Netherlands. Of all the West African countries, Gambia may be the most attuned to traditional tourism. You'll find dozens of luxury beach hotels there whose clientele is primarily British and Dutch. I'd like to spend a few days there recharging my batteries.

Elephant grass grows like mad by the side of the road in Gambia, reaching six to eight feet high. It rustles gently in the breeze. In every little village, children yell *"toubab"*—white man—as I drive by. The road to the capital is full of huge potholes; in some places, the blacktop has vanished altogether. The river is reddish brown, as if millions of automobiles lie there rusting. Where it empties into the Atlantic Ocean, near the little town of Barra, the Gambia is some two and a half miles wide. The capital, Banjul, and the neighboring luxury beach hotels I'm headed for are on the other side. There's no bridge. Just as with the Senegal River, the only way to cross is by ferry. And the ferry isn't running, at least not for the time being. Or maybe it is. The heavyset woman cooling herself with a reed fan in the stuffy ticket office doesn't know for sure. But she's already sold me a ticket.

"Tomorrow maybe," she answers when I ask when I can cross. "But it could be the day after tomorrow."

"Jesus," I say.

She shrugs.

The line of waiting cars winds through Barra's main street. The motorists bring me up to speed. Normally, two boats sail back and forth between Barra and Banjul. One of those boats is being repaired, and now it looks as if the other one has broken down as well. Sometimes it sails; sometimes it doesn't. A few trucks have been waiting three days already, says a driver with a load of cashews. There's not a trace of agitation, anger, or anxiety in his voice. There is only resignation—a resignation that seems to have taken control of all of the people waiting.

Imagine what would happen in a Western country if a ferry that's supposed to run several times a day didn't run for three days. When a ferry's not on time in the West, people start to grumble, grouse, and whine within fifteen minutes. They want to speak to the supervisor, they demand their money back, and finally they leave (anything's better than waiting). If the delay persists long enough—say, a day—reporters from the local newspapers and TV arrive. Everyone, from the public to those in power, calls it a scandal. Fingers are pointed, and heads roll. In any case, resigned faces like the ones I see here are never part of the scene.

The Polish journalist, writer, and Africa expert Ryszard Kapuściński observes in *The Shadow of the Sun*, his collection of essays about the continent, that Europeans and Africans have completely different conceptions of time. According to Kapuściński, "In the European worldview, time exists outside man, exists objectively, and has measurable and linear characteristics. The European feels himself to be time's slave, dependent on it, subject to it. To exist and function, he must obey its ironclad, inviolate laws, its inflexible principles and rules. He must heed deadlines, dates, days, and hours.

"Africans apprehend time differently," Kapuściński continues, conscious that he's generalizing. "For them, it is a much looser concept, more open, elastic, subjective . . . Time is even something that man can create outright, for time is made manifest through events, and whether an event takes place or not depends, after all, on man alone . . . Time appears as a result of our actions, and vanishes when we neglect or ignore it. It is something that springs to life under our influence, but falls into a state of hibernation, even nonexistence, if we do not direct our energy toward it. It is a subservient passive essence, and, most importantly, one dependent on man. The absolute opposite of time as it is understood in the European worldview."

Nowhere do you see these different conceptions of time better than in places where people have to wait. Such as in an African bus station, where Kapuściński arrived at his reflections, or here, at a ferry. To his ever-increasing aggravation, the European sees the clock ticking away the minutes, hours, and days; for the African, those minutes, hours, and days of waiting seem not to exist. He waits, and only comes to life again when the ferry arrives. According to Kapuściński, that waiting is so deeply rooted in the African being that it has resulted in a special physical state of waiting. The waiting of the African is a sort of slumber, a short-lived hibernation whose physiological characteristics the author describes in detail. The waiting African's muscles relax; his body goes limp. His gaze is vacant and indifferent. He doesn't eat, drink, or go to the toilet.

It's not that extreme in the line for the ferry to Banjul.

Some of those waiting are definitely impassive, but at the same time others are making a party of it. Here and there among the cackling chickens and the stacked bags of raw cashews stand women stirring steaming pots. Many people sit on the ground eating or conversing, while little boys run around selling prepaid cell phone cards and little girls peddle doughnuts.

All the white folks have left. Why?

Kapuściński was right. Most Africans do indeed seem to have a different conception of time and, along with that, an admirable disposition for waiting. But why is that? Not even Kapuściński knows the answer.

But isn't there a very prosaic and simple explanation?

Time is money.

Our entire Western way of life is permeated by the idea that time and money are interwoven. Not only in business but even in our free time as well, on vacation. You have vacation only a couple weeks a year, you've paid good money for that trip, and you have a *right* to something nice. You can't afford to sit and wait two whole days for a ferry; that would be a waste. For us Westerners, time has an economic value: it's scarce. We want so much but have so little time for everything. We're supposed to have a career by the time we're thirty. A full agenda is a prerequisite for a successful life. Every minute of our life must have a meaningful purpose. Wasting time, or waiting, is the equivalent of flushing money down the toilet. That's why all those white people have left. They couldn't stand waiting any longer and took refuge in a hotel. Of course, they're still waiting there, but at poolside, taking it easy, and that, it goes without saying, beats two days in the dusty main street of Barra.

For Africans, waiting, instead of a waste of time, is in reality a part of making money. The one does not exist without the other. The *only* way to make money here is by waiting. Waiting for customers who want to buy cell phone cards. Waiting for a tourist who wants to cross the border and will pay you a few bucks if he thinks you can ease the way. Waiting for the ferry to take you across the river so you can sell your chickens and cashews on the other side. Wherever you go in Africa, especially in cities, you find people waiting. Time is something the African has in abundance. He has it to spare.

This "waiting to be able to work" on the part of the African has a pleasant consequence for the visiting Westerner: he never has to wait. Because the Westerner has too little time and too much money, everyone here is always at his beck and call. Should he want his car repaired, for instance, someone is immediately there to help him; should the mechanic by chance be busy with another, African automobile, then he gladly abandons that one for the

Westerner's, which is sure to provide him more money. Where the poor black African always has to wait, the rich white Westerner never does. If I hadn't been traveling by car, I could easily have rented a boat to take me across the river.

Maybe that's why I'm so impatient: up till now, I haven't had to wait. Okay, an hour for my dinner in Senegal, but never more than that. The celebrated African rhythm, that way of life in which haste plays no role, in which stress, as I learned from Abba, does not exist—that African rhythm is still as foreign to me as it was in Casablanca when I didn't have the patience to wait for a visa to Mauritania. I'm still too much the Westerner. Instead of looking at things in the African way, I fall into a sort of European state of waiting, a state characterized by nervous pacing to and fro, deep sighs, and checking one's watch every five minutes. The physiological symptoms are a warm forehead, increased perspiration, and a high degree of agitation.

Dear Jesus, I wonder, do I really have to wait here two whole days?

How would the Scottish explorer Mungo Park have felt here? Park was the first white man to visit the interior of West Africa—and live to tell about it. A little ways upstream on this same river in 1795, he waited no less than five months before he could begin his perilous African adventure. Not for a ferry, it's true, but still.

Park had set out for Gambia at the behest of the Africa Association, a society of wealthy British gentlemen founded in 1788 that had as its object the collection of as much factual information concerning Africa as possible. The Africa Association was mainly interested in West Africa, especially because next to nothing was known about it at the time. The only details considered the least bit reliable came from Leo Africanus, a Moorish explorer who had wandered around West Africa in the sixteenth century. Africanus was a protégé of Pope Leo X (hence his Latin name) and had, during his stay in the Vatican, committed his adventures to paper. For a century, his *Description of Africa* was the standard work on the continent. Apart from Africanus, the rest of the available knowledge about the northern half of Africa came directly from antiquity. The Greek historian Herodotus, for example, spoke of a people known as the Garamantes, whose speech showed more similarities to the shrieking of a bat than to any human language. And the Roman Pliny the Elder wrote of the Blemmyes, headless creatures with their eyes and mouths in their chests. Maps of the eighteenth century, insofar as they weren't figments of their makers' imagination, showed mostly blank spots in West Africa. The Africa Association felt something ought to be done about that. It dispatched a number of explorers with two missions: the discovery of the legendary Timbuktu, where the streets were supposedly paved with gold, and the mapping of the source and course of the just as mysterious Niger River.

A better mission would have been: just try to survive. West Africa wasn't known as the white man's grave for nothing. In the preceding century, every Western explorer who had tried to reach Timbuktu had either been murdered or died of malaria—and the employees of the Africa Association were no exception. Park was the third explorer the association had sent to West Africa. As he wrote in a lighthearted letter to his brother, common sense dictated that he faced certain death. But hoping for fame and fortune, he accepted the mission anyway. "It is a short expedition," he explained, "and will give me an opportunity of Distinguishing myself." The trip from London to Gambia went well, and unlike his predecessors, he somehow managed to avoid immediately falling prey to malaria. Sailing up the Gambia a ways, he stopped to visit the British merchant and slave trader Dr. Laidley, the association's agent in West Africa. There, however, things went wrong. On a beautiful cloudless night he spent gaping at the stars, he was eaten alive by mosquitoes and contracted malaria after all. It was five months before he had recovered enough to leave. It's not known whether, like me, he got irritated by the waiting, or followed the locals' lead and resigned himself to the wait. In any case, he did succumb to boredom. Only conversations with Dr. Laidley brought any relief in "the tedious hours during that gloomy season when the rain falls in torrents, when suffocating heats oppress by day, and when the night is spent by the terrified travelers in listening to the croaking of frogs, the shrill cry of the jackal, and the deep howling of the hyena."

No, it certainly doesn't sound as if Park was a happy camper.

On December 2, 1795, after almost half a year at Dr. Laidley's, Park finally left, wearing a chic blue frock coat with yellow buttons, carrying an umbrella, and sporting a top hat in which he hid the notes of his trip. He must have been quite a sight in the African villages and royal courts he visited.

If Mungo Park could wait nearly half a year to enter the African interior, then surely I can wait two days to catch a ferry, can't I?

No, I can't.

To hell with it, I think.

Carefree luxury and comfort? Forget about it.

I turn my car around. I may not have Mungo Park's patience, but that doesn't mean I can't follow his trail. I head away from the coast and the luxury beach hotels, into the West African interior.

"IT WAS WORN OUT"

Year: 1993
Mileage: 29,760
Price: $9,915
Owner: Hugo Verheyden

The trail of my Benz's former owners seemed to have gone cold. Ronald had led me to Anton, but when I spoke to Anton in Antwerp, he couldn't tell me any more than that the car had supposedly belonged to an old lady.

How would I ever track the former owners down?

At Mercedes-Benz's Belgian headquarters, they destroy all records after ten years. "No idea who your car's owner was," a spokesman said. "Try the DMV."

The Department of Motor Vehicles keeps records of the owner—and past owners—of every car in Belgium. I found an official who wanted to help, but the privacy laws prevented him from just handing me the former owners' addresses. He *was* willing to write a letter to them on my behalf asking them to get in touch with me.

Nobody replied.

A reporter for a Flemish newspaper knew a hacker who could break into the DMV's computers and locate the former owners' addresses. That sounded rather exciting, but a few weeks later the reporter had to admit, "That hacker can't do that anymore."

My car had a decal for a Mercedes dealership in the Flemish town of Lokeren on the back. The dealer said it was possible he might have sold the car new, but he wasn't sure. And he threw his records away after ten years, too. My search was beginning to get frustrating.

But then I received an e-mail from Anton. He'd been talking it over with his brother again, and that story about an old lady, no, that wasn't altogether true after all. His brother had bought the car from a used-car dealer near Brussels. But he had good news. His brother had looked in the attic and found the former owner's Belgian registration. He was a certain Hugo Verheyden from Bierbeek. Unfortunately, there was no Verheyden in the phone book. I sent a letter to the address on the registration—and another one a few weeks later.

No reply.

And now? Now I'm in Bierbeek. And what's that on the mailbox at the address on the registration? The name Verheyden.

The dog barks. I ring the bell. No one comes to the door.

Damn, damn, damn. I trudge slowly back down the driveway in front of Hugo's bungalow to my car. Has my search ended here, in this Flemish village, behind the Catholic church and the bar Sport, where they have Leffe on tap?

Then a man in shorts comes riding up the driveway on a bicycle. He wears thick glasses to which a pair of bushy eyebrows seem to be attached. A baseball cap with the logo of a popular Belgian TV cop series is propped on the back of his head. He's missing three front teeth.

"Are you Mr. Verheyden?"

"Sure am."

I quickly introduce myself and explain why I've come. "Ah, you're that gentleman with the book." So he did get my letters and the one from the DMV. "But I'm not interested in where that car has been and what it's been through," he says, and as far as he's concerned, that's that.

I do my best, fire a few questions at him.

Hugo, a former manager declared redundant during a round of downsizing at the Belgian phone company, owned my Mercedes for six years. He was the car's second owner, having bought it from a friend of a friend. The seller wanted a BMW. He remembers that well: the only reason the man sold his Mercedes was that he'd gotten it into his head that BMW was better. He also remembers exactly how much the first owner had paid for the car: $24,789. Five years later, Hugo paid just $9,915. "You should never buy a car new," he concludes.

He never did much of anything out of the ordinary with the Mercedes, except for driving it back and forth to Spain or Portugal every year on vacation. It was mostly his wife who used the car, to commute to work in the next village. Still, when he sold it, there were 186,000 miles on the odometer. "It was worn out," according to Hugo. The clutch slipped, the shocks needed replacing, the heater didn't work. One day a local car dealer with one of those big flatbed trucks came by and asked if that Mercedes parked in the yard was for sale. He offered five hundred dollars. Like Anton after him, Hugo said he'd "sooner torch it" than sell it for that. The dealer finally bought it for twelve hundred bucks.

The conversation is coming to a close. We're still standing in the driveway, and a cup of coffee for the writer from Holland isn't in the cards. I had assumed that Hugo had had just as emotional a connection to "our" Mercedes as I do. But for Hugo this Mercedes has never been anything more than one automobile among millions of other automobiles. Maybe I'm abnormal having feelings for inanimate objects, but I don't think so. After all, Ronald and Anton had gotten just as attached to this Mercedes as I am. And they both had a story to tell about the car, something that Hugo, no matter how hard I pry, doesn't have. I'm no longer surprised that he never answered the letters.

Meeting Hugo bums me out.

It's as if I'm discovering that a friend I took for an adventurer who had led a fascinating and extraordinary life has been a boring middle-class mook all along. The conversation with Hugo especially depresses me because Hugo, as Pirsig might say, doesn't see the romance of our Mercedes. Hugo takes a classical view of the car. He sees only the underlying form, an ordinary commuter car. He doesn't realize how groovy his old car is. In short, he doesn't appreciate the Quality of the Mercedes.

I don't expect much, but I ask anyway: "Could you maybe put me in touch with the first owner, the man who sold you the car?" Hugo promises to look through his old papers and see if he can find an address. A week later, he actually calls me up. He's found the phone number for Georges van Driessche, a postmaster in Ghent.

NOW I HELP MYSELF

"To date, more than nine million motorists just like you have purchased one of the volumes in the series *Jetzt helfe ich mir selbst.*" So begins *the* self-help book for the German motorist, *Now I Help Myself.* There's a volume for every kind of car on the German Autobahn, including the Mercedes 190 D. That introduction ought to be reassuring. After all, those nine million readers can't all be top mechanics; they must include a few "interested laypeople" like myself. The book promises to make you "self-reliant and competent in all matters concerning your car." But the more I flip through my copy, the more despondent I get. I try comparing the illustrations in the book with what I see before me under the hood. I struggle to make sense of the diagrams and outlines, to understand what's here, but I end up feeling like John and Sylvia in *Zen and the Art of Motorcycle Maintenance.* To hell with all that confounded technical crap. Frustrated, I throw *Jetzt helfe ich mir selbst* in the trunk.

While preparing for this trip, I'd had enough by page thirty, where *regelmäßige Wartung*—regular maintenance—is described. Boring, deadly, dry as dust. Too classical, to use Pirsig's term, not romantic enough. I preferred fantasizing about wild rides through the African savanna amid blaring elephants and age-old baobab trees. As for all the things that could go wrong with my car . . . oh, Mercedes is a quality brand, isn't it?

That laziness is coming back to haunt me now.

First, the brakes gave out. I had to pump harder and harder on the brake pedal before the car would start slowing down. Until finally: nothing. When I braked, it felt as if I were kicking a hole in the air. Fortunately, I happened to be on a really deserted road at the time, somewhere between Kayes and Bamako, the capital of Mali, so there wasn't much danger. Every now and then a herd of long-horned cattle crossed the road, and sometimes a truck loaded so high it looked as if it might tip over at any second rumbled past. The road led through villages with mud huts where children went to school under a tree and where, if you stopped, you were offered a bowl of fresh water drawn from a well in a bucket. They hardly spoke French here, and a white man was still a curiosity. To get my car repaired, I had to get to Bamako.

Then a shock absorber—actually what mechanics call a strut—broke.

The road, being built with the help of the European Union, was still under construction. The embankment for the road was finished, but the road itself hadn't yet been paved. On account of the truck traffic, a washboard piste of the worst sort had developed. The ridges must have been two inches high. Alongside the embankment lay the old sandy piste, which ran through dry riverbeds strewn with boulders. It was a matter of choosing the lesser of two evils. Should I drive over the washboard and hope that nothing broke, or should I opt for the sand and risk getting stuck again and again? As always, I opted for speed. What I'd experienced in the Sahara was child's play compared with this washboard. The road felt like an endless series of icy speed bumps. Every few minutes, I felt the car slip from under me. Jolting and sliding, I barreled toward Bamako at forty-five miles an hour.

What was I doing to my Mercedes?

Suddenly it was over. I heard a loud *thump, thump, thump* like a drumroll coming from the front of the car. The struts had taken such a beating that one of them had broken right through the chassis. I could only continue at a snail's pace. I was still some sixty miles from Bamako.

I've pitched my tent in the savanna a little ways from that damn washboard piste under an enormous baobab tree, and I'm sitting here now with *Jetzt helfe ich mir selbst* in my lap, no brakes, and a busted strut. How am I ever going to get out of here?

I ought to be scared, or at least concerned, I muse, but I'm not. I gather some wood, build a fire, uncork my last bottle of wine, light up a cigarette, and gape at the setting sun, which bathes the baobab and my wounded Mercedes in a magnificent glow. In the distance, I hear drums, singing, and the sounds of a village. The acrid smoke of the fire stings my nostrils, my hands are black with grease, my clothes are stiff with dirt, and I'm happy.

For the first time in a long time.

Maybe I should have sold my car in Kayes yesterday after all. Since I left Senegal, there's been plenty of interest in my Mercedes again. "Is it for sale?" "What do you want for it?" "I have a buyer for you." In the day and a half I spent in Kayes, it drove me crazy. I resolutely ignored every inquiry, not because I didn't want to sell, but on account of a story a Dutch aid worker had told me a few days earlier.

I'd met him at the border between Senegal and Mali. He had offered his car for sale in Kayes last year, he told me when he heard I wanted to sell my Mercedes. In a couple of days he'd spoken to ten potential buyers and finally found one with whom he could do business. The evening of the sale, having unloaded his Mercedes for a good price, he drank a glass of whiskey to the happy ending in the bar of his hotel. In the middle of the night, the cops roused him from his bed and slapped cuffs on him. Not that anyone pays any attention to it most of the time, but selling cars in Mali without paying import duties is officially prohibited. It says that, too, in no uncertain terms, on the laissez-passer, or permit, for the temporary importation of automobiles that they hand you at the border: *"vendre interdit"*—selling prohibited. It soon dawned on the Dutchman that the buyer had cut a deal with the cops and sold him out: from his cell, he could see the man laughing over a beer with the chief of police. He sat in jail three days before they dumped him over the border—without a car, money, or luggage.

No, I better not sell my car in Kayes, I'd thought. But am I so much better off now: stuck in the middle of the bush with car trouble and no means of escape?

All that interest in my car in Kayes *had* piqued my curiosity. How much *would* my Mercedes fetch here? People had told me on numerous occasions that the prices in Mali are the highest in all West Africa. I put the question to Ali, the doorman at my hotel.

"I don't know what a Mercedes costs," he said, peeved. "Poor people don't buy a Mercedes. Poor people know what a bicycle costs, what rice and flour cost, but not a Mercedes." My question had touched a nerve. Ali launched into an inspired speech. "Believe me, we were much better off under colonialism. At least the French knew how to manage things, how to govern a country. Those fat bastards in charge now . . ." Ali left his sentence unfinished, paused for effect, then continued, "All poor people get is a kick in the ass. My boss? Pay? I haven't been paid in months. A boss who doesn't pay is no boss. But what am I supposed to do? If I could, I'd leave for Europe tomorrow, but I have eleven kids; I can't desert them. My oldest son is a doctor, studied in Bamako, but he can't find work here in Mali. You know what he does now? He's a janitor in Libya and is saving up to go to Spain so he can make more money at the same sort of job there. But, um . . . if you're looking for a buyer for that car of yours, I'll ask around."

Kayes is the hottest city in Africa. The *average* temperature in April and May is 108 degrees. In the afternoon you can't do much more than rest and wait until the worst of the heat is over. That's what I did. I lay listlessly on the dingy sheets of a sagging hotel bed, sweat running in rivulets down my naked body, and stared at the cockroaches playing tag on the ceiling—didn't the heat bother *them*? I turned the TV on to a French news channel. Snowstorms had paralyzed large parts of central Europe.

The temperature had become bearable by the end of the afternoon, and I went into town. Within five minutes I had run into a police checkpoint. Police checkpoints in Africa are a bit like stoplights in New York City: there's one on nearly every corner. At your first one, you're still pretty nervous and even a little afraid; once you've been through dozens of them, they're as exciting as a stoplight, too. The African police checkpoint serves no other purpose than to dispel boredom—chat a while with a stranger—and, of course, to see if there's something to be had. Practically every cop asks the traveler for a "gift." What sort of gift is left to the giver's imagination. If you politely refuse, keep smiling, and remain calm, nine times out of ten you can drive on.

But sometimes that doesn't work.

Four men were standing by the side of the road. One blew hard on a whistle; another motioned for me to pull over. A white person in a car with a foreign license plate is always a target. That's not racism; it's common sense: after all, there's something to be had from tourists. Police checkpoints are no fun for the native population, either—African motorists have to pay, too, and for them the expense is much harder to bear than it is for me—but the cops also know that you can't get blood out of a turnip.

One of the cops checked my papers. Finding those in order, he had me open the trunk. Did I have a fire extinguisher? Yes, I did. Did I have a warning triangle? I had that, too. Did I also have a second warning triangle? No, I didn't.

"That's a serious offense, sir," the cop said resentfully, as if I'd personally offended him.

"Is it, now?" I sneered. "Well, that's a shame."

It upset him that I didn't take him seriously. He collected my driver's license, strode to his colleagues, and left me to stew. After five minutes, I walked over to him.

"A second warning triangle," I said. "Now, don't you find that a bit much yourself?"

No, he did not.

"We are going to have to ask you to accompany us to head-quarters," he said, slowly and deliberately.

I thought of the aid worker who sold his car. I saw myself lying in a jail full of shit, rats, and roaches.

"Okay, okay. What's the fine for such a serious offense?" I asked the cop.

"Thirty thousand francs."

Thirty thousand African francs—the African franc, or CFA, is a common West African currency coupled to the euro—is approximately forty-six dollars, about what this cop made in a month. But fines in Africa are like prices in the market. There's room for haggling. What's more, if you don't bargain, you spoil the game. So I joked, quipped, played on his feelings, and pointed out that it was a little strange for him to fine me for not having a second warning triangle when there were people driving around here without any head- or taillights. In five minutes I had him down to seven thousand francs—about eleven dollars. I handed him the "fine."

"You're from Holland, eh?" said the cop, neatly folding his money and then slapping me heartily on the back. "Holland. Good country. My cousin lives in Groningen. Good cars from the Netherlands. You wouldn't want to sell that Mercedes, would you?"

"Yeah, yeah. I mean, no," I muttered, rather taken aback by his sudden good humor.

"Where are you staying?" he asked. "I'll drop by this evening. Maybe we can do business, and I'll buy you a beer. I can afford that now." And he and his colleagues roared with pealing, diabolical laughter. I lied about where I was staying.

Yeah, it was definitely a good thing I didn't sell my car in Kayes.

Meanwhile, I've gotten a little nervous after all. I may be comfortable here by the campfire in front of my tent now, but I'll have to move on again eventually, won't I?

Pirsig says it's important not to start tinkering with an engine "in the direct sun or late in the day when your brain gets muddy."

Pirsig says that most of the problems you experience when tinkering with an engine arise from "failures to use the head properly."

Pirsig says that when one is solving a technical problem, everything depends on making the correct diagnosis. Better a correct, perhaps somewhat simple-sounding formulation of the problem than jumping to conclusions. I feel justified, therefore, in confining myself for the time being to the observation "It's busted"

and waiting until the worst of the heat has passed in order to begin calmly reading my *Jetzt helfe ich mir selbst* by candlelight.

After a few hours' study, I've calmed down a little. I don't have
to solve this myself. I *can't* solve this myself. Not only because it far
exceeds my ability but also because I need new parts. My book
suggests that my brake problem has something to do with a defect
in the brake fluid reservoir, the *Bremsflüssigkeitsbehälter*—I find
that such a beautiful word that I actually hope that the problem
could not have been caused by anything other than the *Bremsflüssigkeitsbehälter*.

And the strut? I manage to diagnose that problem in a classic
rational manner. The strut is held in place by a sort of cap, a rubber mount, in the chassis. That mount is torn, so that the strut
sticks right through the chassis. It has to be replaced. Piece of
cake, according to the manual.

That may be so, but for the time being, there's no Mercedes
dealership or auto parts store anywhere in sight. There's only one
thing to do: get to Bamako. But I don't feel much like going there,
buying parts, and coming back again.

In the morning, when my brain is no longer muddy, I decide to
risk it. If I drive carefully, twenty or twenty-five miles an hour tops,
and if the road remains quiet, I ought to be able to reach Bamako. It
takes me the whole day to cover those sixty miles. I reach the Niger
River that evening just before darkness sets in. "I saw with infinite
pleasure the great object of my mission, glittering in the morning
sun, as broad as the Thames at Westminster," wrote Mungo Park
when he finally saw the long-sought river, a little ways downstream
from where I am now. That infinite pleasure of Park's—I relish it,
too. I can breathe easy now. I've reached Bamako; I ought to be able
to find a mechanic here who can fix my car.

I may have had car trouble in the African interior, but for Mungo
Park the trip from Gambia to the Niger was infinitely more diffi-

cult. His journey was one long series of hardships and depriva-
tions. In every little kingdom (and there were dozens of them in
West Africa at the end of the eighteenth century) he had to cede
a portion of his supplies to the local ruler in order to gain safe passage—the eighteenth-century equivalent of today's police checkpoints, you might say, with the difference that Park really couldn't
get by with just a chat and a smile. It began the first week of his
expedition. During an audience with the king of Bondou, Park offered tobacco, gunpowder, amber, and his umbrella. Unfortunately,
that wasn't good enough for the monarch. He had his eye on Park's
beloved blue frock coat with the yellow buttons. "The request of
an African prince, in his own dominions, particularly when made
to a stranger, comes little short of a command," Park noted drily
in *Travels in the Interior of Africa*. Good-bye, jacket. And it went
from bad to worse. In a principality farther on, in the kingdom of
Kajaaga, asking gave way to taking: in the name of the king,
twenty horsemen stole half of Park's supplies. Later, in Kasson,
half of what he had left was pilfered. Rolling with the punches,
Park endured it all with forbearance; there's not a shred of indignation in his entire journal.

On account of fighting in the west, Park felt obliged to turn
north, in the direction of the Sahara. There, things really went
wrong. In a little village on the edge of the desert, he was taken
captive by the men of a local Moorish ruler named Ali. The reason? Ali's wife, the "remarkably corpulent" Fatima, wanted to see
a real Christian up close. But nearly two months passed before Fatima deigned to meet the prisoner, and in the meantime Park was
taunted, cursed, and starved. His captors debated endlessly
whether to kill him, cut off his arm, or poke out his eyes. All this
made Park, every inch a gentleman, "very melancholy." Sometimes, however, his feelings did surface, such as when he described
the Moors, whom he called the world's rudest savages. Like James
Riley and Saint-Exupéry after him, Park had nothing good to say

about the people: "It is sufficient to observe that the rudeness, ferocity, and fanaticism which distinguish the Moors from the rest of mankind found here a proper subject whereon to exercise their propensities," he wrote. "I was a stranger, I was unprotected, and I was a Christian; each of these circumstances is sufficient to drive every spark of humanity from the heart of a Moor." Meanwhile, the Moors had gotten into a war with their neighbors to the south. During the panic that ensued, Park managed to escape, after nearly four months in captivity, with nothing but the clothes on his back, his compass, and, of course, his top hat, in which his notes were still hidden. A few weeks later he became the first white man to reach the Niger, near the town of Ségou in present-day Mali.

There he found, to his immense satisfaction, that the Niger flowed not to the west, like the Senegal and the Gambia, but to the east, just as he had always predicted. Confident of making enough of an impression in London with that news, he decided to call an end to his explorations of Africa for the time being and head home, leaving the discovery of Timbuktu to the Frenchman René Caillié fifty years later. On the way back, Park stopped in Bamako, which he described as a small, "middling town."

You can't say that about the capital of Mali nowadays. The sky above Bamako is a bizarre blue gray. The downtown is permanently gridlocked with puffing cars and sputtering mopeds disgorging clouds of smoke. Walking offers no relief: the sidewalks, or what passes for them, are also jammed with traffic. Peddlers display their wares there; I constantly have to stop to avoid bumping into somebody. The smell of garbage and excrement rises from concrete ditches alongside the street. The overwhelming heat really makes this tropical cocktail of congestion, filth, and stench complete. Everyone wants to buy my Mercedes—even with the broken strut and defective *Bremsflüssigkeitsbehälter*. You hear cries of "Mercedes!" everywhere. I get so annoyed by all the attention that I tape a sign to the rear window: *"Cette voiture n'est pas à vendre"*—This Car Is Not for Sale.

There's work to be done. Asking around, I manage to find a mechanic, Madi, a friendly thirtysomething. He has Band-Aids on his fingers and holes in his T-shirt, on which is pictured a raised thumb with the legend "Success." Madi has a workplace on the edge of town. I've gotten used to African garages, and this one is no different: wrecks lie here and there, parts are scattered over the oil-drenched sand, a handful of apprentices assist the boss, and a couple of stray toddlers wander around. I spend two days on excursions to junkyards. Madi and I drive around town looking for a secondhand strut and a *Bremsflüssigkeitsbehälter*—my diagnosis turned out to be right.

On my first evening in town, I'm sitting in a cab, a Mercedes 190 D, of course. I tell the driver, Souleymane, that I have the exact same car he does, and that breaks the ice. Souleymane is extremely satisfied with his Mercedes. He used to drive a Peugeot, but that was nothing. True, that Peugeot had everything you need, namely tires, brakes, an engine, and a steering wheel, but *"il mange trop beaucoup de l'argent"*—it ate too much money. Like the son of Ali, the doorman in Kayes, Souleymane worked in Libya a few years. But they were all racists there, so he came back. Bamako is home. He thinks I ought to be able to get three thousand dollars for my Mercedes here in Mali—and that means that he will never be able to buy a car of his own. He rents the Mercedes he's driving now. He has to pay his boss seventeen dollars a day, plus buy his own gas. My fare comes to $2.30. So you have to get at least ten fares a day to break even. That's often all he does: break even. He can't save any money to buy his own car. A bank loan? Forget about it: banks don't loan money to poor people, let alone to cabbies like him.

In principle, I believe in the free-market system. I've brought a Mercedes to Africa because there's money to be made; someone will want to buy my Mercedes to make money with it himself. Everybody will be happy. That's about how I'd imagined it. Only I really don't want to sell my Mercedes to the people who have been interested in it up till now. They're supercilious car dealers, arrogant fat cats, not hardworking small-business men or honest shopkeepers. And all that time I had thought that my Mercedes could provide a man like Souleymane with a decent regular income. Although I faulted Amadou, the mechanic in Nouadhibou, for not being able to set aside a few cents for a new jack, I can hardly blame Souleymane for not being able to save three thousand dollars. That's hardly possible for me, much less for a Bamako cabdriver who, according to him, earns only seventy-five dollars a month. To hear him tell it, his boss is the only one who would make money with my Mercedes, and that man is already rolling in dough. In fact, I reflect in the backseat of Souleymane's cab, it's the same story everywhere: there are capitalists, and there are wage slaves.

I snap out of my funk when we pull up to the Appaloosa, the best bar in town, according to the *Lonely Planet*. Cow horns on the wall, a rough-hewn bar, pennants hanging from the ceiling, country and western on the jukebox—if you didn't know any better, you'd think you were in Indiana. The Appaloosa is packed with white men. Russian girls in tight tops are tending bar. Black women with high heels and lots of makeup chat up the customers.

I order a beer. And another.

Someone taps me on the shoulder. It's one of the three pudgy Germans from the Auberge Sahara in Nouakchott who were on their way to Mali with their Benzes. His friends are here, too. They sold their cars today and are here to celebrate. All three sold to the same trader. For twenty-seven hundred dollars per Mercedes.

"He promised three thousand, but you know how it goes with those guys," screams Christian, the friendliest of the bunch, over

Dolly Parton. "When it's time to close the deal, they never have enough money."

Christian looks sleepy; his breath has the sickly odor of Amaretto. I ask him if he wouldn't have preferred to sell his car to a private individual—a cabdriver, say—who would use the car for himself.

"Get lost," he says. "Whoever's got the money gets it."

Like me, they had car trouble in Mali. "*Scheisse* car. I'm glad I'm rid of it." I tell him about the problem with my *Bremsflüssigkeitsbehälter,* but Christian is more interested in the black woman with the bleached-blond hair and sad eyes who's hanging on his arm.

"Have you ever *gefickt* with the *Mädchen* here?" he asks all of a sudden—Ever fucked a Bamako girl?

"Why, no," I say, taken aback, while staring at his friends, who are looking around bored.

"Shall I arrange one for you?" he offers, scanning the bar for a girl who's free. "They're not expensive, you know. Fifteen bucks for the whole night."

"Don't bother," I stammer. "I prefer . . . you know, I'd rather do it . . . *Ich, ich helfe mir selbst."*

FLEEING, SEARCHING

'm racing the bus. First one of us takes the lead, then the other. It's much better to be in front—you have a clear view, and you don't have to eat the other guy's dust. We're driving on an unpaved road; passing cars kick up clouds of fine red sand. Here and there, the road becomes a washboard piste. My Mercedes may have been repaired, but I'm still a little worried about it. And so I let the bus, which never slows down, go ahead now and then.

Consequently, the bus reaches the border with Burkina Faso just before me. That's annoying: now I'll have to wait until all the passengers are through customs before it's my turn. I'm on my way to Ghana but have to go through Burkina Faso to get there.

The customs office is a bare, windowless concrete room. A tall, skinny man with close-cropped hair stands in the middle, screaming and waving his arms. He has colorful tattoos on his arms, his neck, and even his forehead. He's American, and he reminds me of somebody. But who? Suddenly I see it: the actor Dennis Hopper. The same piercing blue eyes, the wild, manic look. A handful of people have gathered around him. As I walk in, someone whispers to me, "A nut."

The problem is the American doesn't have a visa for Burkina Faso. That's troublesome but not insurmountable. The customs agents have already offered to sell him a visa here at the border.

And that's why he's mad. "Muthafuckers!" he screams. They don't understand him and aren't angry, just upset by his fit. The customs agent in charge slides piles of paper from one corner of his desk to another.

"Then just put it on my credit card, buncha assholes!" he yells, flinging his card on the table.

The head agent picks it up and says in French, "You can't pay with that here."

The American spots me.

"Hey, man, do you know what that fucker's sayin'?"

I step a little closer to him. He stinks of sweat. I translate the agent's words.

"What a fucked-up country this is!" he exclaims. "Buncha savages." And then he turns to me: "What do you make of this shit?"

I say nothing. I want to put my own affairs in order first, have my passport stamped, buy a laissez-passer. But the agents are too upset by the raging American. The head agent asks if I can translate what he's saying. I tell him I don't understand what he's talking about, either.

"Is he on drugs?" the agent asks.

"Could very well be."

"It's a goddamn shame you have to pay for a visa!" the American roars in the meantime. "I don't want nothin' to do with your stupid little country. Do you have the slightest idea how much development aid my country gives your country? You oughta be grateful an American dropped by."

"Give that man ten bucks for that visa," I tell him. "Then we can all move on."

That's oil on the fire.

"I'm not movin' till these muthafuckers let me go. I'll sleep here if I have to."

So it goes, at least one expletive to every sentence.

Suddenly I've had enough. Who does this punk think he is?

"Man, do you know how hard it is to get a visa for your country?" I snap at him. "Do you think these people could ever get a visa for America?" My voice is skipping with rage. "Do you think you could just show up at your country's border, curse out the customs agents, and still buy a visa on the spot? Well? And you stand here whining like a little kid. Just pay that man or fuck off."

Well, that feels good. Moreover, my outburst has an effect, because the man finally shuts his mouth. The head agent stares at me in admiration. The American mumbles a couple of unintelligible words and digs a few crumpled bills out of his pocket.

When we're both outside again, I offer him a cigarette. His fellow passengers are waiting. Everyone's relieved that he's calmed down and that now the bus can leave. The bus driver starts the engine, and the passengers take their seats. The American struggles to the rear and wriggles into place in the backseat, next to a girl who rolls her eyes when she sees him approaching. I notice it and ask the girl through the open window, *"Ça va?"*—How's it going?

She sighs and says, *"Il parle beaucoup!"*—He talks a lot.

"Hey, man, nice talkin' to you!" the American yells. My backpack is at my feet, the *Lonely Planet* sticking halfway out.

"You travel with the *Planet?*" he shouts with obvious disdain as the bus begins slowly pulling away. "Loser!"

The next morning three boys are standing next to my car.

"Where are you from?" one of them asks.

I ignore them. I don't feel like talking. I'm in a hurry, want to get a move on and drive as far as I can before dark. Yesterday, on account of the delay at the border, darkness overtook me. That happens a lot. Dusk doesn't exist in Africa. It's either light or dark. Night falls in Africa as if God in heaven flipped a light switch. Last night, because of the dark, I had to chance it and, instead of looking around for the best place to stay, grab the first hotel I saw, here, just over the border in Burkina Faso.

"Don't you have any work for us?" the same boy persists.

"Shouldn't you be in school?" I counter.

"We don't have any money for school."

I study the boys carefully, ask their names. All three of them are named Alex. Well, okay, to be precise, the oldest is named Alex, the middle one Alexis, and the youngest Alexander. They're fourteen, thirteen, and twelve years old. Alex and Alexis are brothers. Alexander is their cousin. Alex does the talking. His one plastic flip-flop is broken. All African boys have close-cropped hair, but his is a couple inches too long. Alex is on the verge of becoming a beggar. One push in the wrong direction, and he'll join the army of begging ragamuffins you see on every street corner in African cities, an empty look in their eyes and an empty cup in their hands. But beggars do nothing but beg and plead. Alex isn't that far yet. Alex is different. The look in his eyes isn't empty, only deeply sad. This boy can't be fourteen, I think, as I look him over good. He has bags under his eyes like a young father who hasn't slept in months thanks to a crying baby. He's also well-spoken. At the end of his story, he concludes with a line from a song by the great Ivorian reggae star Alpha Blondy: *"Les vrais ennemis de l'Afrique sont les africains"*—The true enemies of Africa are the Africans themselves.

We have a Coke at my hotel's outdoor café. The three Alexes are from the Ivory Coast, which borders on Ghana and Burkina Faso. They walked here. In 2002 the Ivory Coast, once so stable and prosperous, erupted in civil war. Immigrants from Burkina Faso, even if they had lived in the Ivory Coast a generation, were murdered or exiled. After a months-long cease-fire, the war flared up again. In Abidjan, the country's most important city, gangs of xenophobic thugs torched Western schools, raped Frenchwomen, and murdered African immigrants. The whites were evacuated by air; the blacks remained behind.

Alex's father, a native of Burkina Faso, was shot to death in front of his sons by supporters of President Laurent Gbagbo. Alex doesn't know where his mother is. She fled together with his sister. The three Alexes came to Burkina Faso, to this village, where their grandma lives. They'd like to go to school, but they have no money. School costs six thousand African francs, about nine dollars, per person per year. The thought occurs to me that the three Alexes could be three little Abbas. But Alex's precocious look, the resigned way he tells his story, and at the same time the way he longs to be able to go to school convince me of the opposite. No, I believe these boys.

The four of us get in the Mercedes and drive to their grandma's house. The boys love it. They've never ridden in a passenger car. They don't even know how to open the door. The three Alexes' grandma lives on the edge of town in a two-room apartment that looks out on a common, sandy yard. She sleeps in one room; the three boys, in the other. She doesn't speak French and doesn't understand why I've come. Actually, neither do I.

I want to give the money not to the boys but to her so that it will really be used for school. But what difference can it make to me? Who am I to tell this family how best to survive? Grandma makes her money as a street peddler selling medicinal herbs in plastic sandwich bags. The family has no possessions. The boys have the clothes on their backs, a mat to sleep on, and notebooks—each of them has a little pile of notebooks—full of chicken scratches as only boys can make them. I think of my own son, much younger than the three Alexes. His room is three times as big as theirs. He has a closetful of nice clothes, toys he never plays with, and notebooks with chicken scratches just like these.

In exchange for eighteen thousand francs—about twenty-seven dollars—I ask the three Alexes to write me a letter. I ask them to let me know how they're doing in school.

"A letter," says Alex, hesitating. "You have to put a stamp on that."

"Yes," I confirm.

"How much does a stamp cost?" Alex asks.

"I don't know," I say. "Maybe six hundred francs."

Alex looks serious. I see him thinking: A six-hundred-franc stamp, that's 10 percent of my school money. Where will I ever get that?

There's a big color TV in the customs office tuned to the American cable program *Pet Star*, in which house pets and their owners perform amusing tricks. Today's program features a skateboarding cat, a poodle in swim trunks, and a bowling pig that bows to applause.

"Ha-ha-ha-ha-ha. Did you see that?" A chubby customs agent clutches his stomach in laughter. He and a handful of colleagues have been glued to *Pet Star* for nearly ten minutes now—without so much as looking up at me.

I'm at the border again, the Ghanaian border this time, waiting to have my passport stamped.

"Hey, man, wassup?" I hear behind me.

I turn around.

It's the angry American. Please, not again.

"Good to see you, man. Want somethin' to drink?" And he offers me a hip flask of vodka. I politely decline. "Let me introduce you to my friend Stephen," he says, his arms outstretched, his penetrating blue eyes wide open. "This guy has taught me a whole lot about Africa."

Stephen is a Ghanaian in his mid-twenties. Round face, friendly smile. "That was a helluva country, eh?" the American says. "Burkina Faso, I mean. No? Then America. Buncha fuckin' assholes there. I'll never set foot on American soil again as long as Bush is in power. Seriously. America's goin' to hell. Where did you stay? In some shitty hotel from the *Lonely Planet*, no doubt. Ha-ha-ha. Stevie here and I hung out with a crazy girl from the bus, man. We partied, man!"

The angry American isn't angry anymore. What happened to him?

"I owe you an explanation," he tells me a little later when we're outside again. "There at the border you must have thought: What an ugly American. But I'll tell you somethin', man: that was all an act. I met Stephen on that bus. He came from Mali and didn't have any papers. We decided I'd create a diversion so Steve could slip over the border. But how? What should I do? Then it hit me. What does an American do? Why, he complains about money."

I stare at him in disbelief. That scene at the border was an act?

"Tell him your story, Steve," the American says, nudging the Ghanaian with his elbow.

Steve enjoys telling it. He comes from Accra, the Ghanaian capital. It was the prospect not only of wealth, he says, but of adventure as well that made him want to try to get to Europe. He knows lots of guys who've tried. Most give up and return; a few are never heard from again: Did they die on the way, or did they make it in France? No one knows. The idea was to cross the Mediterranean from somewhere on the coast of Morocco or Algeria. Or to climb the fence that surrounds Ceuta and Melilla. He would see.

The trip passed without a hitch until Agadez in Niger. There he met a smuggler who could take him to Libya, where he could make enough money for the next leg of his trip. The man bundled him onto the back of a pickup along with thirty-five other Africans. Just over the border, in the middle of the desert, they had to get out and turn over all of their possessions. "We even had to take off our clothes; they only let me keep my underpants on. The desert was horrible. I saw people go mad with thirst. I drank my own urine." Stephen thought he was going to die. But he kept walking, along with a few others, and they finally managed to reach civilization. He has no idea what became of the rest of the group. After half a year in Libya, he had made enough money. Then, again with a smuggler, it was on to Algeria. The Algerian army caught them crossing the border in the middle of the night in a couple of Land Rovers. The smuggler and his helpers tried to escape. The soldiers started shooting. A Ghanaian whom Stephen had gotten to know was shot in the hand. A boy fell from the first Land Rover and was run over by the second. They left him. Everyone was arrested. After two weeks in jail Stephen was allowed to go. But he had had enough. He didn't feel like continuing; it had gotten too dangerous. And now here he is at the Ghanaian border, hoping they'll let him through so he can get back home. He wants to see his family again. He smiles, confident of a bright future.

Ian and Leslie are lounging in a couple of folding chairs in front of their Unimog, an enormous four-wheel-drive truck made by Mercedes-Benz. That gives us something to talk about. Ian opens an ice-cold beer from his refrigerator for me. The Unimog (from the German *UNIversal-MOtor-Gerät*—universal motor machine) is known for being super solid. Thanks to an ingenious combination of a flexible frame and extremely high ground clearance, the vehicle can handle any terrain. It can ford rivers, drive over boulders, and run through sand. Armies all over the world use the thing. Ian and Leslie have turned theirs into a motor home. There's a kitchen, a chemical toilet, a shower, a bedroom, and a living room. They have electricity, a refrigerator, a color TV, a laptop, and a satellite dish. There's enough food for three months on board and a water tank that holds 132 gallons, the same as the gas tank. They are completely self-sufficient. Only . . . not at the moment. The Unimog is out of commission. Something to do with oil in the wheel bearings. Ian explained it to me, but I didn't really understand it. What I do understand is that the problem is so complicated only specialized German mechanics can solve it.

I've met Ian and Leslie in Ghana's vast Mole National Park, a favorite among tourists because you can see large herds of elephants up close here. Ian and Leslie are a specific type of Africa traveler. They're overlanders, people who drive across Africa in their own vehicle. Like so many, they're on their way to South Africa. Overlanders are usually couples in their early thirties. At home they live in the suburbs, work as consultants, and want to experience one last adventure before they start having kids. They see the routine of the rest of their lives looming and hurry and do something crazy—a trip around the world or to Africa—before settling down for good. They've prepared for their dream trip, or expedition, as they call it, for months, sometimes for years. Colorful decals on the sides of their SUV advertise their expedition's Web site, where they reveal at length how much they've tinkered with their vehicle, what they've brought along, and how much it's all cost. They give their vehicles names like Chuckie, Rover, or Shaggy. A disproportionate number of overlanders are Dutch, perhaps because middle-class life in the Netherlands is so absolute and inescapable. For overlanders, Africa is one big zoo. They get excited only about wild animals and judge the success or failure of their expedition by whether or not they've seen the big five—elephant, lion, leopard, buffalo, and rhinoceros. Conversations with overlanders always involve the same subjects: how terrible the "locals" are, where you should get your visa, how reliable the water is, how bad the roads are, and, of course, how your vehicle is holding up.

Ian and Leslie aren't much different.

"These horrible locals are always begging gifts," says Leslie. "But I can't give everyone something, can I?"

"The BBC World Service used to be a lot better," Ian grumbles.

Ian and Leslie have been driving through Africa for a year. They travel from one national park to another, from one *Lonely Planet* campground to the next, avoiding cities and contact with Africans. What are they looking for here? They themselves don't know. In fact, they're not interested in Africa at all. Ian, a former accountant in his early fifties, recently received a golden handshake from the pharmaceutical company where he used to work. He decided he had worked enough and wanted to begin enjoying life. They bought the Unimog because Ian found it so interesting, and only later did they consider where they would drive it. They chose Africa because there the Unimog would have something to do. "It would be ridiculous to drive such a monster through Europe," Ian says. "But in Africa a machine like this is useful."

The outdoor café at Mole National Park is perched on the edge of a cliff, offering a terrific view of a savanna forest that stretches as far as the eye can see. At the edge of the forest is a little lake where herds of elephants come to drink in the early morning. Next to the café is a tree, and in that tree is a girl of about twenty with short spiky hair, cutoff jeans, and a bikini top. She has her arms wrapped around a big limb. One of the park employees, a black woman with an expression of exhaustion, looks on, shaking her head. She yells at the girl, "Get out of that tree! That's dangerous!"

The girl would rather not. She likes it there. She doesn't think she'll fall. But the woman insists. She's right, of course. She'll be blamed if the girl falls. The girl is right, too: the chance of her falling is negligible. The two discuss the matter a while, but the girl finally climbs down. Her name is Mateja. She hails from

Slovenia and is a follower of the teachings of Rudolf Steiner, at least if I understand her correctly. Her upper body is covered with black spots. "I like getting dirty," she says when I offer her a beer. "The primitive conditions, that's what I like about Africa. Cooking over an open fire, sleeping on the ground, slaughtering a goat. No computers, no cell phones." And a moment later: "You know, in Benin people worship snakes. It has something to do with voodoo. I'm afraid of snakes, really deathly afraid. I have nightmares about them. But I want to get over that. I don't want to live with irrational fears. So I'm going to Benin. Snakes—that's why I've come to Africa."

Claude, a young Frenchman who has just graduated with a degree in engineering, is sitting nearby, wearing flip-flops and an African dashiki. Claude is traveling across Africa by thumb and public transportation—as far as he's concerned, the only way to *really* get to know the continent. Thanks to the air-conditioned SUV that gave him a lift here, he has a bad cold. "I was shivering in that car. Can you imagine? Shivering in Africa." I do find that hard to imagine, I have to admit, but to be honest, it seems to me it would be a relief. I consider the lack of air-conditioning one of my Benz's greatest shortcomings. And I think every African agrees with me, because one of the first things prospective buyers always ask is whether the car has air-conditioning. According to Claude, however, air-conditioning is typical of the way whites travel in Africa. "They sit in their new Western clothes in their expensive Western cars in a cool, artificial Western climate and cut themselves off from the African reality all around them." Claude is going to Mali next month to work for an aid project. He does find it "adventurous" that I've driven to Ghana in an old Mercedes without any air-conditioning, but he also thinks it's decadent. "The people here don't need a Mercedes," he says. "Look at the pollution those old wrecks cause in the big cities. Cars are the West's sacred cows; what they need here are real cows."

The café is starting to jump. More and more people are grabbing seats. Here's the young Dutchman Sebastian, another recent graduate and, like so many grads, clueless as to what to do with the rest of his life. Teaching diving in Thailand—he'd like that. In any case, he's seen Africa. Sebastian has spent the last six months working as a volunteer in the neighboring city of Tamale. More from a thirst for adventure than from idealism, by the way. With his bright yellow formfitting T-shirt, his tanned athletic body, his light blond mane, and his carefree smile, he seems more like a Dutch student on vacation on the Mediterranean island of Ibiza than an African aid worker in the making. The volunteer industry in Ghana is booming. Hundreds of organizations and businesses provide internships and volunteer work here, giving young people the feeling they can do something about the world's problems. Sometimes people pay thousands of dollars to be able to work in Ghana a few months for free. Few Ghanaians seem to have any real need for the work these kids perform. Together with a few other volunteers, Sebastian visited wells and inspected water mains, then wrote a thick report with recommendations. "It'll probably disappear in a drawer somewhere," he says, resigned. "I had a great time with the other volunteers, but I'm not sure I really contributed anything." In any case, in his few months in Ghana, Sebastian has lost all hope of a "better Africa." "People here don't want to work," he says. "At the office, everyone plays solitaire all day on their computer—if they've bothered to show up at all. Hey, no skin off my ass. But why should we give them any money then?"

Olaf is the last to join the crowd. Olaf is a Swedish doctor in training. He's interning in the emergency ward of a hospital in Accra. "Nothing ever happens in a Swedish hospital," he says. "You seldom see gunshot wounds, for instance. If anyone ever came in with really serious injuries, the doctor would get stressed out and nearly go into shock himself." In the hospital in Accra, a whole range of horrible human suffering passes before his eyes: a ten-year-old AIDS patient, the maimed victim of a traffic accident, a pregnant woman with a gunshot wound in her belly. He performs procedures that only the most experienced surgeons in Sweden attempt. Olaf speaks passionately about his job, and yet with the cold, rational detachment peculiar to doctors. Matters of life and death are just work to him. A body is a machine he can patch up provided he has the proper tools and parts. And that's what's lacking in Ghana. More than once he's had a patient die in his arms. Not only because Ghanaians, for lack of money, usually wait till the last possible moment to see a doctor, and thus help comes too late, but also because equipment doesn't work. The hospital is always out of oxygen bottles and drugs; the defibrillator is always broken. "With some extra money, I could save so many more lives."

Sometimes it seems as if everyone I meet, whether Westerner or African, is both fleeing from and searching for something. The three Alexes: fleeing from war, searching for a school. Stephen: fleeing from poverty, searching for wealth. The angry American: fleeing George Bush, searching for adventure. Leslie and Ian: fleeing the emptiness of their middle-class existence, searching for wild animals and beautiful scenery. Mateja: fleeing modern life, searching for a cure for her fears. Claude: fleeing the West, searching for a way to help Africa. Sebastian: fleeing adulthood, searching for a purpose in life. Olaf: fleeing the boredom of his professional life, searching for experience. Africa is—for the Westerners, in any case—a catharsis.

And me? When it comes to fleeing, I'm a little like Ian and Leslie and a little like Olaf. When it comes to searching, a little like the angry American, a little like Sebastian, and a little like Olaf. But above all, of course, I'm searching for *someone*—a buyer for my Mercedes.

THE INDUSTRIAL
UNDERBELLY OF GHANA

The road to Kumasi is the road to the jungle—or what's left of it. Northern Ghana is flat, a sparse savanna. The farther south you drive, the hillier it gets. Palm, pineapple, and banana trees appear; here and there stands a solitary kapok tree, extending to a height of 150 feet or more. Lush nature explodes from every crack and crevice. All that green exuberance takes some getting used to. The stifling smell of overripe mangoes hangs in the air. The dry heat of the savanna has given way to a sweltering humidity that causes sweat to drip from your body even when you're sitting still. My T-shirt has been stuck to the driver's seat all day long.

The road is busy . . . and dangerous.

A truck lies on its side, half its load of pineapples scattered across the road. A little later, I'm driving behind an Opel Kadett, the most popular car in Ghana. The Opel is battered; its one remaining taillight is broken. Someone has painted "GOOD LUCK" on the bumper in sloppy capital letters.

Then something happens that I've dreaded for months. I see an object roll off the road to the left. A hubcap? No, it's not a hubcap; it's a wheel! It skips over the road: boing . . . boing . . . boing. It's the Opel's left front wheel. The Opel itself slides off the road to the left, making a terrible racket.

Brakes!

Miraculously, the Opel remains upright, continuing down the shoulder. *BANG!* It runs into a tree. The driver emerges, dazed. One of the passengers chases after the wheel. The Opel isn't doing so well. The wheel has broken off the axle; half the front end is smashed. In the West, this car would be ready for the scrap heap. Here it's ready for Suame Magazine.

Suame Magazine—Suame for short—is Ghana's scorched industrial underbelly. It's the country's largest automotive repair center—many say the largest in all West Africa. Here, in this suburb of Kumasi, ten thousand mechanics work at keeping the decrepit West African auto fleet on the road. Suame announces itself long before I reach it. I get stuck in a traffic jam of cars of the sort I imagine being patched up again in Suame Magazine. They grumble, growl, and smoke to beat the band. Unrestrained nature gradually gives way to uncontrolled development: gas stations, concrete building frames, corrugated-metal huts, piles of auto parts. As far as the eye can see, piles of auto parts: engines, transmissions, doors, mirrors, hubcaps—every conceivable part for every conceivable vehicle—and all of them arranged in neat rows. Specialization is carried to an extreme here. One used-parts store sells nothing but engines for Mercedes trucks; another, drive belts for Toyota pickups. Jehovah Enterprises specializes in exhausts (and nothing else); One Man No Chop deals in rear axles for Korean cars. At first glance, the area looks like a gigantic auto graveyard, but it's really an auto hospital. Cars don't come here to die; they come to get better.

I leave the highway blacktop and enter on foot the unpaved paths and alleys that lead to the heart of Suame Magazine. Here the area looks like a contemporary African version of a painting by the fifteenth-century Dutch proto-surrealist master Hieronymus Bosch. The sound of hissing welding torches and clanging hammers never stops. Everyone works outside. A bare-chested man gleaming with sweat drags a big piece of metal. Was it once the hood of a car? A cupboard door? His colleague fans a fire with a bellows as big as a large backpack. He sticks an iron bar in the hot coals and begins bending it with a hammer. Five men lie on the ground under a truck in the anthracite gray sand. They're putting an engine from a Renault truck in a model made by the Dutch company DAF. None of the "garages" here has a lift. Modern tools and machines are unknown. A welding torch run by a couple of batteries is the most advanced apparatus; a hammer, the favorite tool. The predominant color is black: the people and their clothes; the earth, from spilled oil; even the pigs rooting for food on the shit-covered banks of a little stream full of black water. Maybe that's why the *"Bruni! Bruni!"*—White man! White man!—of the shouting children sounds so much more frequent and piercing here. This is no place for white people in clean clothes.

Suame Magazine may seem chaotic, but if you walk around a little longer, you notice how efficiently the area is actually organized. There's a corner for every specialty: here are the sheet metal workers; there, the painters; here, the flat fixers; there, the welders. Mechanics are divided according to make of car. There's a Daewoo Street, a Toyota District, a Renault Alley. "We can make anything," boasts Koffi Aboi, a specialist in Land Rovers. I believe him immediately. There are five Land Rovers in his yard, from relatively new to falling apart. He shows me what he's working on at the moment. A Land Rover's starter has failed. Aboi could buy a part like that somewhere, but Land Rover parts, even used ones, are notoriously expensive. "A Korean starter is a lot cheaper," he says. "No, it's not made for the Land Rover, but that doesn't really mean anything to me. I'll make it work." Aboi can perform all sorts of miracles. Moving the steering wheel of a British car from the right side to the left, for instance. That takes him a day at most. The only thing he doesn't like dealing with is modern electronics. He abhors computer-controlled engines. If he gets a customer with a hip, new car, he prefers to yank that computer nonsense out and put an old-fashioned engine in. Makes a modern model like that run great again.

Aboi and his colleagues understand the art of motorcycle maintenance. These are people after Pirsig's and the driving instructor Ruben's own hearts: they manage to achieve the maximum result with the minimum technical means. I'm sorry there's nothing wrong with my Mercedes; I would have liked to experience the Quality they provide.

You'd never know it by driving on Ghana's roads, but the government is genuinely concerned about wheels falling off and other such hazards. The traffic here claims thousands of victims every year; according to some statistics, the traffic in Ghana is an even bigger killer than AIDS. And so the Ghanaian government, like the Senegalese, has prohibited the importation of old automobiles. After all, old cars make for more problems than new ones. Koffi Aboi finds the regulation ridiculous. "For us, a fifteen-year-old car fresh from Europe is as good as new. It can easily last another ten years." The measure hasn't had much of an effect anyhow. Ghanaians in Europe have found a way around it. "They saw those old European cars in three pieces," Aboi explains. "Then they're parts, and those can be imported. We weld the pieces back together again here."

For years, Ghana was ashamed of Suame Magazine's squalor. The government made life even harder for the mechanics, refusing to provide the area with sewers or electricity. Mechanics couldn't get loans. But the last few years the authorities have taken notice of the raw economic power emanating from the area. Suame has been connected to the electrical grid, more land has been made available, and roads have been laid out. "Even the president has been to visit," says George Amankwaah, chairman of the local association of auto mechanics and unofficial mayor of Suame Magazine. Amankwaah is a big bald man with thick glasses. He holds court in his auto parts store, a stuffy shed with a corrugated-metal roof on which the sun beats down all day long. Mechanics walk in and out. Amankwaah has a few words of wisdom for everyone. Once I've waited forty-five minutes, he's willing to receive me as well. He proudly enumerates all Suame Magazine's pluses: Ghana's largest employer, the largest and most efficient automotive repair center in West Africa. But his ambitions extend further. They should be doing more than just repairing cars here; they should start manufacturing them, too. "Why can they make cars in Korea and we can't?" he hollers. "What's missing here is training and money. There's no shortage of ingenuity." In Amankwaah's vision, Suame ought to be Africa's low-tech answer to the sort of high-tech European auto plant I saw in Bremen.

Although I suspect we'll have to wait a while for the first "Made in Ghana" automobile, industrial activity has already begun here. Suame Magazine is full of entrepreneurs. There are businesses where pickaxes, shovels, and iron gates are made. The local university sponsors a workshop that manufactures custom auto parts. I meet a guy who has discovered a real hole in the market. He turns scrap iron into leaf springs, which are used as shock absorbers in trucks and SUVs. They sell like hotcakes.

Environmentalists would undoubtedly detest Suame, and with good reason: the soil is heavily polluted, and drained oil is being dumped directly in the sewer and stream. Yet however noxious and dangerous the situation may be, for the first time in Africa I find myself hopeful about the economic future of the continent. There's energy in the air here. People are working hard and making money. In economic terms, added value is being produced. It is perhaps telling that there's not a single white aid worker anywhere in all of Suame Magazine. Suame runs without any outside help whatsoever, and that gives the people here a measure of self-esteem. They look to the future full of expectations, while in the rest of Africa opportunism and fatalism so often prevail.

As I drive back to my hotel, it starts raining. Rain. It's months since I've seen rain. This is no Dutch drizzle, either. These are big fat drops that pour down from the sky as if God had suddenly jerked the shower on full blast. The wiper beats frantically back and forth but can't clear the water from the windshield. In ten minutes the road is a quagmire. Traffic grinds to a halt. I get out of my car, and within twenty seconds I'm soaked to the skin.

"I LOVED LOOKING
AT THAT CAR"

Year: 1988
Mileage: 2
Price: $21,319
Owner: Georges van Driessche

My Mercedes had rolled off the assembly line in Bremen on April 26, 1988; a week later it stood in the showroom of M. van Winkel in the Belgian town of Lokeren, exactly as the decal on the trunk of my car suggested. That very same day Georges van Driessche dropped by the dealership to pick the car up. It was his first Mercedes, and he was as pleased as Punch with it.

I pass the Van Winkel dealership one afternoon on my way to visit Georges in Lokeren. It's right next to the exit off the highway to Antwerp, wedged between a Texaco station, a giant supermarket, and a McDonald's. It's an enormous dealership, with dozens of gleaming Benzes in the showroom, but otherwise it's no different from Mercedes dealerships in New York, Amsterdam, or Casablanca.

Georges lives less than five minutes away. His redbrick home is on the outskirts of Lokeren, with a

173

view of a pasture full of Belgian blue-and-white cattle. Georges still drives a Mercedes: a dark green C220 with leather upholstery is parked in the garage. When I arrive, Georges, a quiet yet jovial man, is waiting in the kitchen with cookies, coffee—and his good friend Herman Rogier. Herman turns out to have been instrumental in the purchase and sale of Georges's Mercedes.

While sharing some of my photos of Africa, I tell a few anecdotes about my trip with "our" Mercedes. Georges can hardly believe his old car has been all the way to West Africa. I ask him what made him decide to buy a Mercedes back in 1988 anyhow, considering he'd been satisfied for years with a modest Ford Fiesta.

"Mercedes, that's a swell car," Georges says. "Especially at that time, it was still a car that people thought highly of." Prestige, then. Unlike my friends, Georges belongs to the category of people who still consider Mercedes chic, refined, and elegant. But a more important reason, actually, was that his friend Herman also drove a Mercedes. Herman is practically an evangelist for Mercedes; he goes on about the qualities of Mercedes-Benz for a full hour. He's bought seven new Benzes in his life, all from the same dealership: Van Winkel in Lokeren. After so many cars, Herman is a master at the game of squeezing every last cent of savings out of a car dealer. The trick: haggle, haggle, haggle. He tells at length how they succeeded in wrangling a 7.5 percent discount off the list price on the purchase of Georges's Mercedes. Seventeen years after the fact, Georges and Herman are still proud of their bargaining. Georges even produces the original bill of sale to prove he's not lying: he paid $21,319, not $24,789, as Hugo Verheyden claimed.

Like Hugo, Georges has always stayed close to home. He really drove his Mercedes only to work—Georges was and is a postmaster in Ghent—less than twenty miles away. So after five years, there were only about thirty thousand miles on the odometer. Because a provision in the Belgian tax code encourages people to buy a new car every five years, he sold it then.

Herman was enlisted for the sale, too. Herman knew a colleague, Hugo, who was looking for a relatively new used car. Hugo came to Lokeren one day with his wife, his father-in-law, and $9,915. They took the Mercedes for a test drive. The deal was closed the same evening, and the Mercedes disappeared to Bierbeek.

And what became of that BMW that, according to Hugo, was the reason for the sale?

"I did indeed start driving a BMW," Georges says with regret. Once again, Herman was the instigator. Herman wanted to buy a new car that year, too, but Mercedes didn't have anything he liked. So they made the switch to BMW together. Big mistake. Herman held out barely a year; Georges, a little longer. But after a few months both wanted nothing more than to return to driving their old familiar make again. Georges regretted the sale, especially on days when he was in Bierbeek and saw his old car standing in Hugo's driveway unwashed.

"I washed that Mercedes of yours every week," he says, still a little indignant at Hugo's lack of concern for the look—or, as Pirsig would say, the immediate appearance—of his Mercedes. "I was really addicted to that," Georges says wistfully. "I loved looking at that car."

DEPRESSING BANALITY

On a dingy wall in the Togolese embassy in Accra, the capital of Ghana, hangs a poster with twenty fuzzy photos of all the members of the cabinet of Togo's ex-president Gnassingbé Eyadéma. *"Le Nouvel Exécutif Togolais"*—The New Togolese Administration—it says in big letters at the top of the yellowed placard. That Eyadéma—Africa's longest reigning dictator—died the previous week is obviously of little concern to the embassy staff. The mood in the Togolese embassy isn't the least bit tense; in fact, it's listless. An old TV is tuned to a French-dubbed German soap, *Nicht von schlechten Eltern* (Nothing to Sneeze At). A salamander crawls across the wall. Though a rickety fan does its best to bring a bit of relief from the tropical heat, the sweat runs down my temples and back. In all, three people are waiting for a visa to Togo, among them an American backpacker with a hip-hop hat and a fringe of whiskers. The fact that a coup has taken place in Togo in the wake of President Eyadéma's death is news to him.

"Oh, maybe it's not too safe there then?" he mutters.

I'd thought of that myself. Following the death of President Gnassingbé Eyadéma, a former wrestling champion who never appeared in public without his sunglasses, the Togolese army decided that Eyadéma's son, Faure, should succeed his father. The constitution was changed the very same day, and Faure Eyadéma was the new president of Togo. But that didn't sit well with the public, which had been fed up with the elder Eyadéma for quite some time. His thirty-eight-year rule had been characterized by the usual dictatorial mix of intimidation, murder, empty promises, and a disastrous economic policy. Riots broke out in the capital, Lomé, last week. The army shot and killed a few demonstrators. In Ghana they're preparing to receive a flood of refugees. The Ghanaian army has been placed on alert, and the papers have been screaming bloody murder for days. The Dutch State Department has joined in the hysteria and issued a travel warning. The Dutch embassy is strongly advising against travel to Togo.

Okay, but what should I do? Sell my Mercedes here in Accra? The prices here are bad, and besides that, I'd have problems leaving the country: officially, I'm not allowed to sell my car here. Should I drive back the way I came? I don't feel like that at all. Or should I just take my chances? It helps that Togo is a small, narrow country—about as big as the Netherlands and Belgium put together. From border to border, it's only about thirty-five miles. If need be, I can drive to Benin, the country on the other side, in an hour. I slip twenty thousand African francs (about thirty dollars) in my passport to expedite my visa application a little, and a few hours later the ambassador himself hands me my visa.

"Isn't your country a little dangerous right now?" I ask.

"Pas de problème," he replies.

Yeah, right.

Actually, I'm just naturally curious about the situation in Togo. An African country where a coup has just taken place—that evokes images of tanks in the streets, looting soldiers, burned-out houses, stone-throwing youths, and a terrorized population. How much of that will I get to see? Full of expectations but with my knees knocking, I show up at the border crossing between Ghana and Togo the following morning. The actual border consists of a frayed rope raised and lowered by hand. A few goats root around for scraps. A boy pushes a handcart loaded with bags of onions. Women with bowls of tomatoes on their heads walk by. At the customs office, just as at the embassy, they haven't yet bothered to remove the state portrait of the old Eyadéma.

The border between Ghana and Togo doesn't differ one iota from all those earlier border crossings. There's the hustler who volunteers to help me fill in the forms. There are the customs agents who shamelessly beg for a "gift." And there is the big book in which my personal information is scrupulously recorded. I had been warned that the authorities would take advantage of the situation to rob me blind. But I'm aware of neither excessive greed nor menacing aggression. The only sentiment among the customs agents is, as always, boundless boredom.

Once over the border, I arrive before long in the capital, Lomé. I drive around the city, go for a walk downtown. So this is how a West African country feels after a coup: as if nothing had happened. The country's only newspaper, the state-published *Togo-Presse*, opens with a report on the annual bookkeepers' convention that took place in Lomé yesterday. The stores are open; the people move about freely. Street vendors try to sell me bootleg DVDs and leather belts. But there's not an agitator or a soldier in sight. The only sign of the army I notice is a few stray vehicles near the presidential palace.

Still, you can't say the recent events leave the public cold. On the contrary. You need only order a cup of instant coffee on the street for the conversation to turn immediately to the country's new president. "Togo is a republic, not a kingdom," says a café owner, Jean, from behind his shaky counter, which is piled high with cans of powdered milk emblazoned with the picture of a Dutch milkmaid. "If Papa dies, you can't just appoint Sonny Boy president." Jean plans on demonstrating against the new president next weekend. He's not worried the army might use force to intervene, but he seriously doubts his voice will be heard. "Thanks to pressure from the other West African countries, elections have now been promised. But next they'll be endlessly postponed. That's what's always happened before. Nothing ever changes here."

I stay at the restaurant-inn Chez Alice, named for the proprietor, an elderly bleached-blond Swiss woman who has lived in Togo twenty-six years. Chez Alice is the informal meeting place of the extensive German-speaking community in Lomé. Because the Prussians colonized "Togoland" for a brief period in the nineteenth century, Germany is one of the few European countries with an embassy here. Togo was a favorite vacation destination among Germans in the 1970s and 1980s, and many have stayed. The menu at Chez Alice is in German, and the prices are in euros. Swiss political magazines lie on the counter. According to Alice, the reports of riots and refugees during the coup were grossly exaggerated. "I didn't notice anything," she declares.

Everything in Togo is redolent of past glory. You should have been here twenty, twenty-five years ago, I hear from many a sad-looking German at Chez Alice. Togo was cosmopolitan, prosperous, and optimistic about the future then. It called itself the Switzerland of Africa—maybe that's why Alice settled here. While socialists and communists were wrecking the neighboring countries' economies, the free market in Togo was in its heyday.

Goods entered the port and were shipped on to the rest of West Africa.

No group better epitomized Togo's prosperity then than the famous Nana Benz, market women, often illiterate, who had cornered the market in batik. In West Africa batik is synonymous with *Wax Hollandais*, or Real Dutch Wax, a fabric manufactured by the Dutch company Vlisco. Vlisco has been the undisputed market leader in West Africa since the nineteenth century, and Real Dutch Wax enjoys unprecedented popularity here. There's not a single woman who doesn't either already own a dress made of Real Dutch Wax or dream of owning one. For years, all Real Dutch Wax entered West Africa via Lomé, and the Nana Benz controlled the trade. That trade was so lucrative that the Nana Benz were the first in Togo who could afford to own a Mercedes—hence their nickname. Sometimes they even loaned the president their Benzes for state visits. They soon moved into other businesses, too—the car trade, for instance—and at one point the Nana Benz controlled 40 percent of all the commerce in Togo.

With the devaluation of the African franc, the removal of trade barriers in Ghana, Benin, and Nigeria, and a series of economic crises in Togo, decline set in. There are no longer any Mercedes-Benzes in Lomé's Grand Marché. Real Dutch Wax is still sold there, the rolls of batik are still piled high, but business is bad. The Nana Benz haven't had a monopoly on Real Dutch Wax in a long time. "Nana Benz? They don't exist anymore," snaps one of the market women. A new generation has come up, the Nanettes, who can't stand Mercedes. If they can afford a good car, they'd rather have a BMW, for, as one Nanette put it in a local paper, "Mercedes is a brand of depressing banality."

There is also little left of that other pillar of the Togolese economy: the trans-Africa auto trade. When the route through Algeria was still the most popular, Lomé was the favorite destination of many a Western European car trader. Once you'd conquered the Sahara of Algeria and Niger, it was but a short distance to the magnificent beaches of Togo. The traders chilled out here and disposed of their cars. There are still plenty of reminders of that time—the walls at Chez Alice are lined with European license plates—but only an occasional Western tourist arrives with his own car these days. No one dares drive through Algeria anymore on account of terrorist attacks, and Lebanese traders offer cars at such rock-bottom prices in the port of Lomé that it no longer pays to sell your car here. Helmut, a bearded sixtysomething, has been coming to Togo for twenty-five years. This winter he arrived with a Mercedes delivery van that he finally had to sell at a loss of five hundred dollars.

"The Lebanese have totally cornered the market here. I don't know how those people do it," he grumbles, "but they sell cars for less than what you pay in Germany." He suspects that the Lebanese are using the car trade to launder money. "It's not too hard to sell cars if you don't have to turn a profit."

Seated on heavy oak chairs around the *Stammtisch*, or regulars' table, Alice and her German expatriate clientele discuss the current political climate. "I'll get by, no matter what," says Alice. "Honey, I've been here so long, and I've experienced so much. I'll survive this, too." Fritz, a dealer in African art, isn't worried, either. "Ach, Africans . . . It's always something here, and always nothing."

Then Michel comes in. Michel is a heavyset, moonfaced Togolese fiftysomething who once studied medicine in Munich and speaks flawless German. He's a member of Eyadéma's party. "They're calling it a putsch," he scoffs. "I call it a sensible decision. The army saw Eyadéma as their father, as their leader. With his death, things could easily have gotten out of hand. Without a leader, the army could have bolted and started looting. But no, the army said: We have confidence in Eyadéma's son. Let's appoint him to keep the peace. I don't think that's such a bad idea. And apart from that, these people have been in power for thirty-eight years. To hand over everything at the drop of a hat—well, that's not easy. It's only human, isn't it, to try to hold on to what you have?"

At eight o'clock, Alice turns the TV on for the news from TV TOGO, the only available channel, controlled by the Ministry of Information. The news opens with the brand-new president's visit to Nigeria, which has threatened military intervention if Eyadéma junior doesn't resign. But the news doesn't mention that. Instead, TV TOGO shows the president emerging from his plane, awaited by a delegation of no fewer than fifty men, all of whom are seen shaking the president's hand. Then the report cuts to a continuous minutes-long shot of a conference hall where all the dignitaries have gathered. The item concludes with the farewell at the airport, where once again we witness the president shake everyone's hand. There's not a word on the content of the talks.

Alice erupts in uncontrollable laughter. "Ha-ha-ha. They're good at shaking hands. Nothing's happened again, of course."

JOHNNIE WALKER FOR THE SECRETARY OF TRANSPORTATION

It could have been so much easier. That's what I think when I see the *Grande Africa* moored in the port of Cotonou, Benin's most important city. The *Grande Africa* is a square, monstrous colossus, a so-called Ro-Ro ship. Ro-Ro ships are specially made for the transport of automobiles: "Ro-Ro" is short for "roll on, roll off," and that's exactly what the cars do. Proud ocean liners they're not; rather, Ro-Ros are floating parking garages.

The *Grande Africa* is wedged between a Danish container ship and an Indian freighter. The ship is full of used cars from Western Europe picked up in the ports of Hamburg, Antwerp, and . . . Amsterdam. If I'd put my Mercedes on the *Grande Africa* there, it would have arrived in Cotonou three weeks later—instead of the nearly three months I've spent getting here.

Nowhere in West Africa do so many used cars arrive in one place as here, in the port of Cotonou. In the mid-1980s the trade consisted of a few thousand cars per year; by the beginning of the century, that had risen to 200,000. The whole economy of the city revolves around the car trade. Or revolved, because here, too, things haven't gone so well the last two or three years.

I'd like to tour the port, but that's easier said than done.

A Dutch friend of mine, the one whose wedding in Ouagadougou I attended and who lives in Benin nowadays, has put me in touch with a part-time car trader named Raimi Gado. My friend assured me I could make good use of his services. I called Raimi yesterday, and he was already hard at work on my "case." He told me he'd arranged a meeting with the secretary of transportation for the next day (today). Raimi's uncle was a cabinet member for a brief time, you see. I told him I really wasn't all that interested in the secretary of transportation, but Raimi impressed upon me that I had to start at the top and work my way down.

That was yesterday. Now I drive my Mercedes to Raimi's house in a suburb of Cotonou.

"You can't show up at the secretary of transportation's office like that," mutters Raimi, a gaunt man with a Charlie Chaplin mustache, when he sees my (admittedly!) muddy car. While we're soaping the Mercedes down, Raimi says we have to pick up a bottle of Johnnie Walker—Black Label—somewhere: "The secretary loves good whiskey."

We arrive at the Department of Transportation a couple hours later, driving a clean car and carrying a bottle of Johnnie Walker. The secretary is sitting behind a big desk with five telephones, two of them cell phones. After Raimi and the secretary have spent five minutes inquiring after each other's health and family, Raimi explains that I'd like to tour the port. The secretary nods and reaches for one of his phones. No one asks me anything.

"I have a couple of friends here," he says into the phone. Not journalists, not people, but friends. Friend of a cabinet member— my initial indifference toward the man has vanished. I'm glowing inside. "Could you help them? No, I don't know exactly what they want. I know the one well; the other is an expatriate, an intellectual." I'm curious how he came to that conclusion, but I don't get the chance to ask him. Raimi has already stood up. The secretary scribbles something on his business card.

"This should do the trick," he says, handing the card to Raimi, who accepts it as if it were a five-hundred-dollar bill. Raimi walks to the door, beaming. Meanwhile, I've still got that bottle of whiskey in my bag. I nudge Raimi in the side and gesture with my eyes. He doesn't get it. What do I do with that bottle? I don't dare give it to the secretary here. He'd take that as an insult for sure. Or would he? Maybe I should just leave it with his assistant—with the secretary's secretary, in other words—I think as we close the door behind us. Raimi doesn't like that idea. He doesn't trust the girl. We decide to keep the bottle: the port director, our next stop, will need stroking, too.

The director is watching TV—a French soccer match. "Would you like something to drink?" he asks as we come in. He turns to the refrigerator behind his desk. "Beer or Coke?" I order a Coke; he helps himself to a Heineken.

"To your health," says the director.

The director isn't interested in the reason for my visit, either. "Go see the harbormaster," he says, turning back to the soccer game. Once outside, I realize we've forgotten about the whiskey bottle again.

The harbormaster, dressed in a colorful uniform of Vlisco Real Dutch Wax print, does want to know why I've come. That we've been to see the secretary of transportation and the port director means nothing to him. A tour of the port? That's complicated; it can't be done just like that. First, a special document has to be produced. He checks his computer for a model. Once he's found one, he grabs a pen and a sheet of paper and begins carefully copying it. That takes him twenty minutes. Then he gives the paper to his secretary, who types the document up on her computer. Meanwhile, the harbormaster inspects my car. I have to remove all my luggage from the Mercedes; only empty cars are allowed in the port. "I'll walk," I offer, but Raimi has long since figured out what the man's driving at.

"Gimme that bottle," he whispers. He goes for a stroll with the harbormaster and returns in five minutes. "Not enough," he says, dejected. I give Raimi ten thousand francs—about fifteen bucks—and he slips it to the harbormaster in the hallway.

Suddenly we can leave.

Unfortunately, it's already too late. I had wanted to see them unload the *Grande Africa,* but in the meantime they've all but finished. Most of the cars are already on the wharf; only a few "tow jobs" remain on board.

I've seen the *Grande Africa* once before, just prior to leaving for Africa.

It's a cold November morning, and the *Grande Africa* is lying at one of Amsterdam's western docks, not far from the motocross track where Raoul and Ruben taught me how to drive in sand. A gray Toyota van is parked on the wharf. Werner grabs an iron bar and smashes the passenger-side window. He's not interested in the vehicle's contents, which look like they've been picked up off the street: an old gas stove, two ancient TVs, a couple of lawn chairs, a sink, a musty carpet, and a pile of bulging garbage bags. Still, the cargo must be worth something to the owner, for both the rear hatch and the sliding doors to the cargo compartment are firmly welded shut. Meanwhile, the alarm is going off. But the earsplitting *weeoo weeoo weeoo* doesn't stop Werner. He calmly picks the remains of the glass out of the window frame, sticks his arm inside, and opens the door.

"Ya gotta tell the whole story, okay?" he urges me. Here it is then: Werner is no car thief—although many a car thief could learn a thing or two from him. It's Werner's job to see that the hundreds of used cars parked on the wharf are ready to drive. The keys are supposed to be left in the ignition with the doors to the passenger cabin unlocked. But sometimes people forget and lock the doors, and then Werner has to break in. Sometimes, as in this case, the car won't start, either. After giving it a couple of tries, Werner tilts the front seat forward so that he can reach the battery, which is located not under the hood in Toyota vans like this but in the cabin itself. He takes out a couple of jumper cables, attaches them to the battery, and again tries to start the van. The engine coughs and sputters, but it still won't turn over.

"A tow job," Werner concludes.

That's when Werner's colleague Cees springs into action—or actually, his converted Ford Taurus, which is equipped with a special bumper wrapped with rubber mats. Its vanity plates read "DE SLEEPER," which is misspelled Dutch for something like "DA TOW." "Get in," says Cees. "I'll show you how we tow a van like this to the top." Cees is skinny as a rail, and his face is covered in grease. His left hand holds a burning cigarette; his right rests lightly on the wheel. He tears across the wharf at more than forty-five miles an hour. The Toyota van, tethered by a towrope, jolts along behind. We drive into the *Grande Africa*'s belly. The ship consists of four decks connected by ramps. We need to get to the top level. While Cees, still one-handed, steers the Taurus upward through all sorts of dizzying curves, the Toyota van skates precariously along the walls of the ship. To my amazement, it reaches the top without a scratch. Does anything ever go wrong? I ask.

"Ah, it's all old junk anyway, isn't it?" Cees says, then adds after a pause, "Yeah, sometimes something does happen. You should come here in the winter when it freezes a few degrees. Then it's a skating rink." Once he's delivered his load, a couple of crew members lash the van down. By the time they're finished, Cees is already below again to pick up the next car.

The cars in the *Grande Africa*'s belly look rather naked. No one knows exactly where it happens, but every car dealer is aware that anything not riveted to the car stands a good chance of disappearing under way. That's why doors are welded shut and mirrors, headlights, moldings and trim, and often even whole dashboards are removed from the cars by way of precaution and shipped separately.

Fortunately, not all the cars are tow jobs. There are all sorts of vehicles parked on the wharf: gleaming Benzes, battered Opel Astras, a Rotterdam city bus (Line 5 to Marconi Square), trucks, and even a backhoe. Werner manages to get most of them started without too much trouble. The most common problem is a dead battery. Werner starts the cars, and a handful of drivers stand by to drive them into the ship. The men loading the *Grande Africa* today remind me of cattle drivers. The parking lot full of long-in-the-tooth cars is like a herd of cows—a herd of sacred cows that need not prodding but starting; a herd that needs to be driven not into a corral but onto a ship. The trick is to do that as quickly as possible. And so these Dutch cowboys transform the wharf into a racecourse. Nothing like peeling out with smoking tires—the smell of burned rubber wafts over the wharf all morning long.

A ship full of used cars for which no one in Holland has any use anymore leaves the port of Amsterdam nearly every week. The ships start out from Hamburg, pick up cars in Amsterdam and Antwerp, and then sail for West Africa, where they stop in Senegal, Liberia, the Ivory Coast, Nigeria, Cameroon, and Benin. It's estimated that Europe sends West Africa a half million cars a year, good for sales of about a billion dollars.

The international trade in used cars is constantly in motion. One year, most of the cars go to Africa; the next year, Eastern Europe; the year after that, the Middle East. Hardly any used cars were exported to Iraq under Saddam Hussein, because Iraqis had to pay thousands of dollars in import duties for every car. After America ousted the dictator in 2003, however, the import duties were lifted, and almost all the available Western European used cars disappeared to Iraq that year. In Africa, trade with Liberia and Sierra Leone was interrupted by civil war; now lots of cars go there. The Ivory Coast was always an excellent market but has fallen out of favor since 2003.

You need only stroll Amsterdam's wharves to appreciate just how global the trade in used cars really is. Everyone's familiar with the German company Adidas making sneakers in China or the American company General Electric moving its call centers to India. But this, too, is globalization. The cars were made in Japan and Germany and have driven all over Europe. The *Grande Africa*'s home port is Palermo, Italy; its crew is made up of Russians and Poles. That sounds beautiful, but you can also look at it another way: the trade flows predominantly in one direction— from Europe to Africa. For those enormous Ro-Ro ships in which thousands of Western European cars disappear return from Africa practically empty. All they bring back is a few piles of hardwood logs . . . and, of course, a handful of stowaways now and then. Ben, who has worked in the port of Amsterdam thirty-six years and is responsible for keeping tabs on the number of cars loaded in the *Grande Africa*, knows all about that. "Sometimes there are illegal immigrants in ships like this. It's easy for them to hide." He points out where he's found refugees in the past. There's room for a few people in an open space under the ship's gang-plank. "The guys recently spotted a heap of clothes lying there. They thought: Hey, that's strange, what are those clothes doing there? Turned out not to be clothes at all, but three of those fellas from Africa. Man, what came out from under that gang-plank wasn't a pretty sight."

Back to Benin. There's no Ford Taurus for the tow jobs in Coto-nou. Muscle power alone suffices. Here, five men push the cars that won't start out of the *Grande Africa*. All the unloaded cars, running or not, wind up on an adjoining sandy lot to await re-moval from the port. "There's a lot of theft here," Raimi confides. Last year someone stole an onboard computer out of one of his cars—the shameless thief later tried selling the thing back to Raimi. The dealers try to get their cars out of the port as quickly as possible, therefore, to the car market on the edge of town.

A Benin car market reminds you of a prison yard. It's an enor-mous walled parking lot. The walls are topped with barbed wire, and every fifty feet is a thirteen-foot-tall watchtower made of used lumber and corrugated-metal roofing. The car dealers man their towers like prison guards, looking out over their cars and their cus-tomers. If you see something you like, you have to climb a rickety wooden ladder to negotiate with the seller.

Every imaginable automobile is for sale here: mid-class cars and minivans; station wagons, SUVs, and limousines; European, American, and Japanese cars; Benzes, BMWs, Toyotas, Hondas; even Volvos and an occasional Saab, makes I've never seen in West Africa. The only thing they don't have here is brand-new cars.

I visit the tower of the Lebanese dealer John. Just as in Lomé, the trade here is mostly in the hands of the Lebanese, who, like the Indians, have often lived in Africa for generations. In addition to selling used cars, the Lebanese often run supermarkets or restau-rants. Negotiations with John, a heavyset man with a full beard, happen lightning fast. He names a price; the buyer makes an offer; John, a counteroffer. So it goes, back and forth, one or two more times until John won't budge another cent. John runs the business with his brother in Belgium. The brother takes care of the supply;

he handles the sales. But sales have dragged lately. The past three years were bad enough; the last few months he's considered throwing in the towel a number of times. He can't give his cars away. He's happy if he makes a hundred bucks on a sale these days. If he could sell a few more cars a day, that would be okay. But he can't. Often, a week goes by without a single transaction. The other dealers aren't doing any better. John's near bankruptcy is the rule rather than the exception.

What's wrong with this picture? How can the car business in Benin be so big and at the same time so unprofitable? The Dutch anthropologist Joost Beuving, who studied the car trade in Cotonou for a year and a half, has an explanation. The business's boom years are over, but most car dealers don't want to face it. According to Beuving, the remarkable growth of the trade in the port of Cotonou seems to prove the free-market capitalists right. After all, when all sorts of trade barriers were lifted in Cotonou, the business exploded. Hordes of fortune seekers descended on the car trade. Now that things aren't as good, these same free-market capitalists reason, those hordes ought to disappear. But they're not disappearing. They're continuing to deal, despite mounting losses. According to Beuving, that's because Benin's car dealers are living with the irrational hope of someday clinching a big sale that will make good all their losses in one fell swoop. That reminds me of American day traders who buy and sell the same share dozens of times a day, or Las Vegas gambling addicts, but in a paper in the *Journal of Modern African Studies* Beuving compares Cotonou's car trade to the California gold rush of 1849. Like the first forty-niners, the first car dealers in Africa made enormous profits. Just as in the gold rush, the party ended as soon as thousands of fortune seekers showed up. Just like the forty-niners, Benin's car dealers stubbornly cling to the belief that the old times will return. And there's another parallel: in the end, the only people who do make money, whether it's the gold rush or the car trade, are not the people chasing the dream but the ones who cater to them. During the gold rush, it was the smart guys who provided food and lodging; in the car trade, it's the ship owners, the port authorities, the market owners, and, of course, the brokers.

There's no one John hates more than the brokers who operate at Cotonou's car markets. It works like this: A customer arrives at the gate of a car market, but even before he can enter, he's approached by a broker who just won't leave him alone. Like the hustler at the border, the car market broker earns his keep by "helping" the customer. He sizes up the merchandise, negotiates the price, and navigates through the bureaucratic jungle of rules and regulations. In return, the broker receives a commission from both the buyer and the seller.

According to John, brokers only get in the way, and their bartering only drives the prices up. Their services are superfluous, but he can't afford not to pay them. If he doesn't pay, they won't bring him any customers. Moreover, it's risky to get brokers on your bad side. "They'll slash your tires," John claims, "or they'll beat you up on your way home at night."

To hear John tell it, the life of a car dealer is one big vale of tears. He barely makes a profit, is robbed, cheated, and intimidated. The irrational hope that things will someday be better can't be the only reason he carries on, can it? Indeed, there is something else involved. According to Beuving's study, the Lebanese actually aren't so terribly interested in making a profit at all, let alone in the car business. What motivates them instead is the exciting life of the expatriate. Beuving paints a picture of young adults who want nothing more than to escape the oppressive family ties and rigid social conventions of home. They immigrate to West Africa in hopes of a carefree life full of booze and broads. And though there's little to be made in the car trade, there's still an ample supply of women and drink. "It's really hard to meet girls in Lebanon," says John. "A girlfriend just for sex? Forget about it." In Cotonou, however, that's not a problem. John boasts of his many different *petites amies*, or girl-friends. His religion—he's a devout Christian and has a couple of devotional pictures hanging in his watchtower—doesn't get in the way of that, incidentally. "Of course at some point you have to get married," he says. And that future wife? She, no doubt, will have to be Lebanese.

CARS, MONEY, BROTHERS

Year: 2005
Mileage: 148,180*
Price: $2,400
Owner: . . .

North . . . to Ouagadougou.

If this had been a road movie, then it would have ended here, in Cotonou, on the beach, with a prolonged shot of the ocean lapping at the shore while the credits roll. But this is no film, and the end of the story—the sale of my Mercedes—is still to come. I shouldn't sell it here in Benin—that much is clear after John's sad stories. The prices are higher in Ouagadougou, and maybe the driver of that Mercedes cab from Holland is ready for a new one . . .

---

*Ronald wasn't far off in his estimate that his Mercedes had in reality traveled 300,000 or 400,000 miles, rather than 136,400. The odometer was turned back the first time at 186,000, after Hugo sold the car to a dealer. When Anton's brother bought it a few months later, half those miles had disappeared. Anton himself said he drove the car nearly 75,000 miles, and yet the odometer read only 124,000 when Ronald bought the Mercedes. According to my estimate, at the moment I sell it, the Mercedes has traveled at least 285,000 miles.

Thousands of manioc roots line the side of the road to Burkina Faso. The hot asphalt acts as an oven to slowly bake them dry. It's quiet, except for the occasional truck piled high with bales of cotton. The harvest has just ended; here and there—on the berm, in the cashew trees, among the bushes—lie tufts of cotton. If the African heat were ever to leave your thoughts for even a second, you might imagine they were the last remnants of a thick blanket of melting snow.

It's smooth sailing from Cotonou to Abomey to Parakou and then to the border of Burkina Faso. The jungle recedes, making way again for sparse savanna. I drive through nature parks, through villages with castle-like mud huts with little towers and drawbridges, past the ramshackle palaces of the Abomey kingdom. I let it all pass from behind the window of my car. I drive on, stopping only for hitchhikers, who stand beside the road here in throngs but never go any farther than a few miles.

And for that sheep—I stop for a sheep.

My brakes squeal. THUD. Shit, what's happened to that thing?

This is something else I've been dreading: a collision with an animal. I've had so many near misses—chickens, donkeys, dogs, cows, goats, and sheep—that I thought the Mercedes had become immune to animals. And then it happens at the last second after all. It's mostly goats and sheep you see on the road. Goats are smarter than sheep. They react to the sound of the car. By aiming at their rear, you can guide them a little. But sheep—you can't anticipate what they'll do. That was the case with this one. I noticed it too late, and it made an unexpected move.

I get out. The animal is lying on its side, but it's not dead. It looks around, a little dazed. Then it clambers upright, stamps with its feet as if it wants to test whether everything is still working, and toddles away. A few villagers who came running at the sound of my screeching brakes look on, amused. There's a dent in my bumper.

Two and a half days later I'm in Ouagadougou, which everyone calls Waga for short. The city makes a bad first impression. Interminable, half-built suburbs ring the outskirts, and the road downtown is a long-drawn-out assemblage of phone centers, food vendors, and secondhand auto parts stores. Still, although Ouagadougou looks at first like every other capital in West Africa, it is nonetheless different. There's more life here, more fun, more enjoyment than elsewhere. The cafés and restaurants are packed. I see an overweight woman in a colorful dress of Vlisco Real Dutch Wax print maneuver through traffic on a clattering motor scooter with a bowl of bright red strawberries on her head. Little boys sell plastic bags full of fresh, delicious yogurt. Ouagadougou even has a film festival, the biannual Fespaco, which attracts huge crowds.

But I let the pleasures of Ouagadougou pass.

I go in search of a buyer for my Mercedes.

It's not long before I've found three candidates.

Antonio is a gaunt, nervous kid who works as a guide. He takes tourists on trips through West Africa. He always has to rent a car to transport his clients, and that costs him too much money. So he's looking to buy. He's heard lots of good things about Mercedes.

"It's a reliable car," Antonio says.

I agree.

"I want a car that's just arrived from Europe," Antonio says. "Those are good. Once a car's been driven around on African roads for a few years, there's nothing left to it."

Antonio doesn't have many clients. Or much money. He offers 1.4 million francs, about twenty-one hundred dollars. A nice amount, but he doesn't have it at his disposal. He shows me a letter from an Italian friend who promises to transfer twenty-five hundred to his bank account. But the bank doesn't know anything about it. Antonio begs me to sell him my car.

Jean is an auto broker. I'm standing at my hotel's bar drinking a beer one evening when he comes up and offers his services. He wears dreadlocks and a knit Rasta cap. Actually, he works as a broker only on the side. He's primarily a filmmaker and can no doubt use some extra cash. I promise him 5 percent of the sale price if he brings me a good customer.

And then there's CMB, a car dealer. CMB stands for "Cars, Money, Brothers." CMB got the abbreviation from *New Jack City* by Mario Van Peebles, in which a drug gang called *Cash* Money Brothers appears. That doesn't inspire much confidence—someone who's named himself for a drug gang—but CMB *is* the only one with money. CMB, a small man who talks a lot and very fast, has a big bulge in his right pants pocket—a thick roll of bills. He riffles proudly through the wad of cash with his thumb and forefinger.

CMB runs a used-car dealership on the edge of town. He has about thirty cars for sale on a dusty lot. They're primarily midclass French and Japanese models. He doesn't have a single Mercedes 190, the most popular car in Ouagadougou. When I drive onto the lot, a dozen men immediately surround the car. They open the hood, test the CD player, and start the engine. But the interest in the mechanical condition of my Mercedes extends no further than that. No one asks for a test drive. Whether the brakes work, the transmission is sound, or the car handles the road well— it all leaves CMB and his employees cold. People here seem solely interested in the outward appearance of my Mercedes. They appear to care only about the romance and the groovy aura, not about the underlying form. That surprises me. I'd expected exactly the opposite.

"Why's the Mercedes 190 so popular here?" I ask CMB.

He shrugs. "I tell my customers: Get a Peugeot, that's just as well built," he says. "But no, they just have to have a Mercedes. They think they've got it made if they drive a Mercedes."

The haggling begins. I start at 2 million francs in order to end at 1.6—about twenty-four hundred dollars, twice what I paid for my Mercedes. I come down quickly, but CMB won't go any higher than 1.4 million.

Then my phone rings. It's Jean. He has a buyer for me: a cabbie who's looking for a new Mercedes 190. He's willing to pay 1.7 million.

"One point *seven*?" I yell so loud in my phone that CMB has to hear it.

I tell Jean that the cabbie can have the car if he's really got the money.

When I hang up, CMB makes his final offer: 1.6 million, exactly the amount I want.

CMB has already begun counting out the money on the hood of the car.

"Whoa, whoa," I cry.

He looks at me astonished. "We agree on the price, don't we?"

He assumes the deal is closed, but it's all going a bit too fast for me. My luggage is still in the car, I explain. I need the car this weekend. I offer every excuse I can think of. We finally leave it that I'll return on Monday.

When you tell people you're going to drive an old Mercedes to Africa to sell it there, you basically get three different reactions. Many find it adventurous ("How exciting, tearing across Africa in a car!"), some think it's scandalous or even immoral ("You're gonna scam those poor Third World people with a wreck like that?"), but most actually just don't get it ("What do those people there need with a Mercedes anyway?").

Of course, I'm after adventure. Sure, I'd also like to make something off the car. And no, I don't find that immoral. But the whole thing really revolves around something else . . .

Automobiles are controversial. They're controversial in the West, and they're controversial in Africa as well. African automobiles are usually in bad shape, have a relatively high level of carbon monoxide emissions, and are used in cities that are already dealing with serious environmental problems. So some people view the trade in these polluting machines as a bad case of the West dumping its garbage in the Third World. We're rid of our old junk; the mountain of garbage in Africa just keeps growing. European environmental agencies agree with this assessment. They regard cars that are no longer in running order as refuse. And you can't just export refuse; special, extremely difficult-to-obtain licenses are required for that.

Strangely enough, you never hear Africans talking about such things. They seem to have no problem at all with our refuse. Moreover, there's a real need for our junk, and they're willing to pay good money for it. That, of course, is because what we see as junk can frequently still last years in Africa. Cars often land on the scrap heap in Europe because the repairs needed to keep them on the road are too expensive. But in Africa labor is ridiculously cheap, and it's worth the trouble to fix cars that would be scrapped in Europe. As I learned at the auto repair center Suame Magazine in Ghana, Africans have absolutely no problem whatsoever with cars that aren't in running order. They get them up and running in no time.

It's true that automobiles cause a ton of misery in the world, but they are just as capable of alleviating it. In Africa the automobile allows small farmers—and the majority of the population works in agriculture—to increase the size of their market and therefore their income. Wherever you go on African roads, you always meet an overloaded pickup: farmers on their way to market to sell their tomatoes, carrots, or goats. And what's true for the small farmer is also true for industrial agriculture. The cotton I saw lying by the side of the road a few days ago could never have been grown and transported on such a large scale without the automobile. The pineapples in Ghana, the strawberries here in Burkina Faso—they're unthinkable without automobiles.

Cars are also used more intensively here than in the West. The typical look of a highway in Europe or North America, an endless procession of vehicles with only one occupant apiece, is unimaginable in Africa. Driving by yourself is considered antisocial here. If you've got room, you give people a lift. Most cars here are used not as private vehicles but as public transportation. In the average African city, three-quarters of the cars are cabs.

So I have no scruples at all about the trade in used cars. In fact, I believe car traders in Africa are making a valuable contribution to the economy. I think it's only logical that those traders, like myself, don't care to dispose of their cars for a mere song. Like everyone else in the world, they're out to maximize their profits. That is, after all, the reason they bring the cars here. If there were no profit to be made, then you wouldn't find any car trade here, either—or any cars. I think that Africa is ultimately better served by fair trade than by any sort of development aid.

If all I cared about were business, then the decision wouldn't be so difficult. I would immediately sell my Mercedes to CMB, a fellow car trader. But I want more. What I really want from selling my car here in Ouagadougou is to provide one person a better life, to improve the *Quality* of his or her existence.

At the end of *Zen and the Art of Motorcycle Maintenance*, Pirsig tells how you can achieve Quality in yourself, in things, in your life: through gumption, by which he means bold, enthusiastic resourcefulness. According to Pirsig, you should, above all, be passionate about your motorcycle's maintenance. If you're enthusiastic about what you do, Quality will come of its own accord. That's true not only for motorcycle maintenance but for all the work people perform as well. If you approach life with gumption, you produce Quality. And if everyone produces Quality—the baker, the politician, the auto mechanic—then the world becomes better of its own accord. It may sound like advice from a cheap self-help book, but that doesn't bother me. I totally agree with it.

It had already become clear to me during the tour of the Mercedes plant in Bremen that my car was made with gumption. I myself have driven it with a considerable amount of gumption the past few months. I want to sell my Mercedes to someone who will be as enthusiastic about driving it as I have been, who will use this car with gumption and in so doing experience a better Quality of life.

Who's it going to be? The poor devil Antonio? Jean's customer, a cabdriver like the one I'd always imagined selling my Mercedes to? Or the car dealer who can pay cold, hard cash?

The obvious candidate is the cabbie. I have an appointment with Jean for tomorrow to meet his man. I've resolved to sell him the car, even if it's for half the amount I had in mind. But Jean doesn't show.

I call Antonio and ask him to meet me at my hotel. He drops by a few hours later. He still wants the car. But yeah, that money. I tell him he can have the car for his first offer, 1.4 million francs, but I want the money by Monday morning. In the meantime, I've bought a ticket to Amsterdam; I fly to Paris Monday evening. Antonio swears to me that he'll have the money.

On Monday, Antonio is nowhere to be found.

There's nothing else to do: off to Cars, Money, Brothers.

Over the weekend, I ran into Mateja, the tree-limb-hugging Slovenian girl from Mole National Park. She's tagging along now with a bunch of rather scary-looking ex-Yugoslavians with close-cropped hair, wraparound sunglasses, and muscular bodies. I ask Mateja and one of her friends, Jure, who could pass for the twin brother of Anton Cena, the Mercedes owner from Kosovo, to accompany me. I don't trust CMB.

CMB still has that bulge in his pants pocket. He's glad to see me. Yeah, he's still prepared to pay that 1.6 million. We go to his office, and he begins counting out the bills. Mateja counts them a second time. I chat a little with CMB. Jure stands guard outside.

Once the money has been counted and recounted and the sales contract signed, CMB starts in about customs charges, import duties, and taxes. Here it comes, I think. Here comes the big double cross. Or a small army of cops ready to arrest me, a goon squad that beats me to a pulp, counterfeit money maybe. But he only looks at me with big, pleading puppy dog eyes. I peel two ten-thousand-franc notes from my thick wad of bills—about thirty bucks—and hand them to him. Then everything's settled, and we can leave.

I'm pleased to have maximized my profits, but have I also succeeded in my ambition to use my Mercedes to give some African a qualitatively better life? The answer: perhaps.

If I had waited longer and looked harder, maybe I could have found somebody who I thought *deserved* my Mercedes. But then again, maybe not. Pirsig says that good motorcycle maintenance begins with the proper tools. If you don't have the proper instruments at your disposal, your gumption suffers and you can't achieve any Quality in the maintenance of your motorcycle. Now that I've taken leave of my Mercedes, I no longer wish to view it as a groovy, romantic car. It's time to take a cold, analytic look at the vehicle. I now wish to see my Mercedes as a boring, classic tool. A tool with Quality, to be sure. I just have to trust that the

Benz's Quality will also lead to a qualitatively better life for the new owner, whoever that may be.

Here's what I know: A friend of mine leaves for Ouagadougou a few months later. I ask him to look CMB up. I want to find out who bought the Mercedes. "That turned out harder than I thought it'd be," my friend says when he returns. "CMB didn't trust me for a second. He thought you wanted your car back." Within two weeks of our deal, CMB had resold my Mercedes. He didn't know much about the buyer: he was an African man, not from Burkina Faso, probably from Mali. And the price? He remembered that, of course. CMB had sold my car for 2.2 million francs, almost thirty-four hundred dollars. For less . . . my Mercedes was not for sale.

ACKNOWLEDGMENTS

I left Amsterdam with my Mercedes 190 D in December 2004 and arrived in Ouagadougou three months later. After selling my car, I flew back to the Netherlands via Tripoli and Paris in a matter of hours, and somewhere between Ouagadougou and Amsterdam my luggage disappeared. Fortunately, I had most of my notes in my carry-on bag, though I was still missing a notepad or two. I returned to Africa, therefore, in the summer of 2005, again with a Mercedes 190 D, but this time with my family. I have cobbled these two trips together in this one book, with the footnote that the second trip turned out to be only a minor supplement to the first.

I want to take this opportunity to thank not only everyone named in the book but also others, behind the scenes, who were just as important. First of all, there is Gerbert van der Aa, who took me to Africa for the first time, taught me how to sell cars there, accompanied me on the above-mentioned second trip to West Africa, commented on the book's manuscript, and was an inexhaustible source of knowledge about the Mercedes 190. Without him, this book would not have been written. Henk Nugteren and Hindatou Amadou, whose wedding in Ouagadougou constituted the beginning of this book, also deserve special mention. Henk supported me in both word and deed both before and during my trip and was so good as to let me recuperate in his house for a few days. Jim Schilder and Laurens Ubbink read earlier versions of the book and had many suggestions for improvements. Martijn de Waal rode part of the way with me on the first trip. Special thanks to my translator, John Antonides, who suggested I try to find an American publisher for the book, and to my agent, Felicia Eth, who made the idea a reality. In conclusion, for help and support along the way, I thank Gert van Bergeijk, Nick van Bergeijk, Bertie van Bergeijk-Van der Aa, Tijs van den Boomen, Marnix de Bruyne, Niama Nango Dembélé, Souleymane Diouf, Huub Dubbelman, Tilly Hermans, Marijke Nagtegaal, Mamadou Santo, Liz Waters, and Abdoulaye Zorome. Remke de Lange was, as always, indispensable, from the initial organization of my thoughts to the preparations, the travel, and finally the writing.

Jeroen van Bergeijk
Amsterdam

BIBLIOGRAPHY

In addition to countless Web sites and articles from newspapers and magazines, I have made grateful use of the following books:

Africa on a Shoestring. 9th ed. Footscray, Australia: Lonely Planet Publications, 2001.

Bowles, Paul. *Their Heads Are Green and Their Hands Are Blue.* New York: Random House, 1957.

Cassou, Marcel. *Le transsaharien: L'échec sanglant de Missions Flatters, 1881.* Paris: L'Harmattan, 2005.

Conrad, Joseph. *Heart of Darkness.* New York: Penguin, 1999.

de Botton, Alain. *The Art of Travel.* London: Penguin, 2003.

De Villiers, Marq, and Sheila Hirtle. *Sahara: The Life of the Great Desert.* London: HarperCollins, 2003.

Durou, Jean-Marc. *L'exploration du Sahara.* Paris: Actes-Sud, 2002.

Fleming, Fergus. *The Sword and the Cross.* London: Faber and Faber, 2003.

Haardt, G.-M., and L. Audouin-Dubreuil. *Raid le Citroën: La première traversée du Sahara en automobile.* Paris: Plon, 1924.

Kapuściński, Ryszard. *The Shadow of the Sun.* New York: Alfred A. Knopf, 2001.

King, Dean. *Skeletons on the Zahara.* London: Heinemann, 2004.

Korp, Dieter. *Jetzt helfe ich mir selbst, Band 110 Mercedes-Benz 190 D.* Stuttgart: Motorbuch, 2002.

Langewiesche, William. *Sahara Unveiled: A Journey Across the Desert*. New York: Vintage, 1997.

Lindqvist, Sven. *Desert Divers*. London: Granta Books, 2002.

Morocco. 4th ed. Footscray, Australia: Lonely Planet Publications, 2001.

Nöther, Werner. *Die Erschliessung der Sahara durch Motorfahrzeuge 1901–1936*. Munich: Belleville, 2003.

Park, Mungo. *Travels in the Interior of Africa*. London: Eland, 1983.

Pirsig, Robert M. *Zen and the Art of Motorcycle Maintenance*. New York: Bantam, 1984.

Porch, Douglas. *The Conquest of the Sahara*. New York: Fromm International, 1986.

Riley, James. *Sufferings in Africa*. New York: Lyons Press, 1965.

Rogers, Jim. *Adventure Capitalist*. New York: Random House, 2003.

Saint-Exupéry, Antoine de. *Le petit prince*. Paris: Gallimard, 1999.

———. *Terre des hommes*. Paris: Gallimard, 1972.

———. *Wind, Sand, and Stars*. New York: Harcourt, 1992.

Sattin, Anthony. *The Gates of Africa: Death, Discovery, and the Search for Timbuktu*. London: HarperCollins, 2004.

Schlegelmilch, Rainer W., Hartmut Lehbrink, and Jochen von Osterroth. *Mercedes*. Köningswinter, Germany: Ullmann/Tandem, 2004.

Scott, Chris. *Sahara Overland*. 2nd ed. Hindhead, U.K.: Trailblazer Publications, 2004.

Urry, John. *The Tourist Gaze*. 2nd ed. London: Sage, 2002.

Webster, Paul. *Antoine de Saint-Exupéry: The Life and Death of the Little Prince*. London: Macmillan, 1993.